JOHN ADAIR'S 100 GREATEST IDEAS FOR EFFECTIVE LEADERSHIP AND MANAGEMENT

Successful management and leadership have never been a greater challenge. Managing and leading are not the same thing. Both of course are crucial.

Whether you are a first time manager or an experienced leader, straightforward, practical advice on best practice is hard to find – especially from a proven expert.

John Adair is an internationally recognized writer, teacher and management consultant. He has had a varied and colourful career including work as a hospital orderly in an operating theatre, as a deckhand on an Icelandic trawler and as adjutant of a Bedouin regiment in the Arab Legion. He developed the 'manager-leader' concept that helped ICI become the first British company to make £1 billion pounds profit and his ideas have helped millions of managers worldwide to grow themselves and their organizations. Now *John Adair's 100 Greatest Ideas For Effective Leadership and Management* will help you find the answers and inspiration you need. It provides accessible advice from one of the world's best known and most sought after authorities on leadership and management – advice you can start to put to work in your organization today.

JOHN ADAIR'S 100 GREATEST IDEAS FOR EFFECTIVE LEADERSHIP AND MANAGEMENT

JOHN ADAIR'S 100 GREATEST IDEAS FOR EFFECTIVE LEADERSHIP AND MANAGEMENT

CAPSTONE

The right of John Adair and Neil Thomas to be identified as the authors of this book has been asserted in accordance with the Copyright, Designs and Patents Act 1988

First published 2002 by
Capstone Publishing Limited (a Wiley Company)
The Atrium
Southern Gate
Chichester
West Sussex
PO19 8SQ
www.wileyeurope.com

Reprinted June 2004, December 2004, October 2005, September 2006, January 2007

CIP catalogue records for this book are available from the British Library and the US Library of Congress

ISBN 13: 978-1-84112-140-6 (PB)

Typeset Integra Software Services Pvt.Ltd, Pondicherry,India. www.interga-india.com
Printed and bound by CPI Antony Rowe, Eastbourne

Contents

Preface   *xiii*

Part One: Getting Your Act Together   *1*

Introduction   2

Nine Greatest Ideas for Managing your Time   3

Idea 1 – The Adair ten principles of time management   3
Idea 2 – The five worst traps to avoid   5
Idea 3 – Carry out a time audit on yourself   7
Idea 4 – Identify long-term goals   10
Idea 5 – Make medium-term plans   12
Idea 6 – The Adair urgency/importance matrix   15
Idea 7 – Delegate efficiently   17
Idea 8 – Make use of committed time   20
Idea 9 – Manage your health and avoid stress   21

Five Greatest Ideas for Organising your Office Work   25

Idea 10 – How to deal with interruptions – five techniques to keep them brief   25
Idea 11 – How to deal with paperwork and save an hour of time every day   25

Idea 12 – Five organising ideas to improve time management   26
Idea 13 – How to manage meetings   26
Idea 14 – Recognise the Adair five types of meeting   27
Summary and follow-up test   29

Part Two: Understanding Leadership   *31*

Introduction   32

Five Greatest Ideas for Understanding the Functions of Leadership   34

Idea 15 – Task, team and individual   34
Idea 16 – Leadership function – action-centred leadership   36
Idea 17 – Leadership characteristics – task element   38
Idea 18 – Leadership characteristics – team element   39
Idea 19 – Leadership characteristics – individual element   40
Summary and follow-up test   40

Part Three: Performing As A Leader   *43*

Introduction   44

Three Greatest Ideas for Setting and Achieving your Objectives   45

Idea 20 – Draw up a personal profile   45

Idea 21 – Set personal goals   46
Idea 22 – Set professional business goals   47

Twelve Greatest Ideas for Decision-Making   50

Idea 23 – Refine your decision-making skills   50
Idea 24 – The decision-maker as effective thinker   51
Idea 25 – The manager as decision-maker   53
Idea 26 – How to avoid the trap of compromise decisions   55
Idea 27 – How to use analysis in decision-making   55
Idea 28 – The role of synthesis – a holistic approach – in decision-making   56
Idea 29 – The role of imagination in decision-making   57
Idea 30 – The role of conceptual thinking in decision-making   58
Idea 31 – The role of intuition in decision-making   59
Idea 32 – The role of originality and innovation in decision-making   59
Idea 33 – The concept of value in decision-making   60
Idea 34 – How to weigh up the options in decision-making   61

Nine Greatest Ideas for Leadership Skills   64

Idea 35 – Leadership skills – defining the task   64
Idea 36 – Leadership skills – planning   66
Idea 37 – Leadership skills – briefing   68
Idea 38 – Leadership skills – controlling   70
Idea 39 – Leadership skills – evaluating   71
Idea 40 – Leadership skills – motivating   74
Idea 41 – Leadership skills – organising   75
Idea 42 – Leadership skills – setting an example   78

Idea 43 – The Adair short course on leadership 79

Five Greatest Ideas for Teambuilding 81

Idea 44 – Teambuilding – the functions of the leader 81
Idea 45 – Achieving the task – with a team 84
Idea 46 – Building the team 84
Idea 47 – Developing the individual 85
Idea 48 – The individual and teams 87
Summary and follow-up test 89

Part Four: Thinking As A Leader 93

Introduction 94

Thirteen Greatest Ideas for Creativity and Innovation 95

Idea 49 – Seven obstacles to creativity 95
Idea 50 – Ten things a creative person ought to be 96
Idea 51 – Seven ways to stimulate creativity 97
Idea 52 – The four main stages of creativity 98
Idea 53 – Innovation: the seven key players 98
Idea 54 – How to recruit and retain creative people 100
Idea 55 – How to encourage creativity 101
Idea 56 – How communicating can reinforce innovation 102
Idea 57 – Overcoming obstacles to creativity and innovation 103

Idea 58 – Making your organisation good at innovation   104
Idea 59 – Checklist for the innovative organisation   107
Idea 60 – Ways to generate ideas in an organisation   109
Idea 61 – Using brainstorming to generate ideas   111

Three Greatest Ideas for Leadership Qualities   **115**

Idea 62 – The 25 attributes of leadership and management   115
Idea 63 – The seven qualities of leadership   116
Idea 64 – Leadership qualities test   117
Summary and follow-up test   118

Part Five: Power Through The People   *121*

Introduction   122

Sixteen Greatest Ideas for Getting the Best from your Team   **123**

Idea 65 – Adair's eight rules for motivating people   123
Idea 66 – 50:50 rule of motivation   124
Idea 67 – Maslow's hierarchy of needs   125
Idea 68 – McGregor's theory X and theory Y   126
Idea 69 – Herzberg's motivation-hygiene theory   127
Idea 70 – Manager's motivating checklist   130
Idea 71 – Ten ways to strengthen your own motivation   131
Idea 72 – The seven indicators of high motivation   132

Idea 73 – Choosing people with motivation – the Michelangelo motive   132
Idea 74 – The key to motivating: treat each person as an individual   133
Idea 75 – Using Jacob's ladder to set realistic and challenging targets   135
Idea 76 – Give feedback to reinforce and motivate   136
Idea 77 – Maintain morale to maintain motivation   137
Idea 78 – Create a motivating environment   139
Idea 79 – Give fair rewards to the motivated   139
Idea 80 – Give recognition to the motivated   141
Summary and follow-up test   142

Part Six: Getting The Message Across   145

Introduction   146

Twenty Greatest Ideas for Effective Communication   147

Idea 81 – Adair's 15 key issues in communication   147
Idea 82 – Personal communication skills checklist   148
Idea 83 – Listening – a key element in communication   149
Idea 84 – Being a better listener – developing listening skills   151
Idea 85 – Reading skills – must, should and might   151
Idea 86 – Writing skills – talking to a person on paper   153
Idea 87 – Churchill's guidelines for report writing   155
Idea 88 – Test written reports for effectiveness   155
Idea 89 – Adair's six principles of effective speaking   156
Idea 90 – Profile the occasion – the first element of a good presentation   157
Idea 91 – Plan and write the presentation   159

Idea 92 – Use visual aids in presentations   160
Idea 93 – Prepare your talk – don't prepare to fail   161
Idea 94 – Rehearse a presentation   161
Idea 95 – How best to deliver your presentation on the day   162
Idea 96 – One-to-one interviews   163
Idea 97 – Seven ways to give criticism   164
Idea 98 – Seven ways to receive criticism   164
Idea 99 – Communication and the management of meetings   165
Idea 100 – Communication within your organisation   168
Summary and follow-up test   169

Index   *173*

*P*reface

John Adair has had a major impact on leadership and management development. His practical and applicable ideas have, for example, underpinned the teaching of leadership in particular in the armed services throughout the world.

This book takes a logical look at those issues which an individual has to get to grips with if he or she is to perform well as a manager or leader.

To be successful as either, you have to be: well organised and disciplined; good at goal setting and focused on objectives; able to think creatively and to make decisions; and able to lead, motivate and communicate with other people.

The ideas presented here are a distillation of John Adair's greatest tried and tested ideas on all these areas and will help you to function better as a leader or manager: able to get results through people and able to understand yourself and others.

The book does not debate at length the differences between being a manager and being a leader – the approach is rather that these Greatest Ideas will serve to improve an individual's personal performance both as manager and leader.

Neil Thomas
Editor

Part One

Getting Your Act Together

Introduction

Great leaders and managers are well organised and are able to make the best use of time to achieve desired results. This section of the book analyses the key ingredients needed in 'getting your act together', which will ensure that you manage your time to maximum effect.

Nine Greatest Ideas for Managing your Time

Ask yourself

Do I always make the best use of time? What can I do to save time and spend it wisely?

Idea 1 – The Adair ten principles of time management

Time management is about managing your time with a focus on achievement: of doing and completing those things that you want to do and which need doing.

Time management is goal-driven and results oriented. Success in time management is measured by the quality of both your work and your personal life.

Tempus fugit

Whilst it is true to say that life only makes sense in retrospect, it can be shaped by your sense of time and purpose. In keeping with business planning, *time* planning – and your approach to the use of your time (and to the extent that you can influence it, how others spend their time) – should be to avoid the *trap of failing to plan* – which is, in effect – planning to fail. In other words, if time is money, spend it wisely.

Basic approach to time management

You need to be certain that you:

- can define your business role and know what constitutes a successful outcome;
- spend time thinking and planning for yourself and others;
- have a clear understanding of your business purpose; and
- know the balance you wish to achieve between your business and your private commitments (and can identify the time demands on both).

Remind yourself

Time management skills should be applied to your personal life as well as your business life.

The Adair ten principles of time management

1 Develop a personal sense of time.
2 Identify long-term goals.
3 Make medium-term plans.
4 Plan the day.
5 Make the best use of your best time.
6 Organise office work.
7 Manage meetings.
8 Delegate effectively.
9 Make use of committed time.
10 Manage your health.

Idea 2 – The five worst traps to avoid

At all costs you should avoid being one of the following stereotypes:

- *A poor delegator.* Delegating can save you time and develop your staff. You should delegate as much as you can.

Ask yourself

Why am I not delegating?

- *A bad organiser.* Bad organisers think that they are busy, but they are not. They are snowed under by paperwork, constantly interrupted and complain that there are not enough hours in the day.

Ask yourself

Do I know what I have done today and what I have achieved?

- *An excellent procrastinator.* You should not put off doing something that should be done. If you are doing this intentionally, habitually and reprehensibly, then you are a procrastinator.

Ask yourself

Why am I putting this off?

- *A poor performer at meetings*. Lack of preparation and poor control waste valuable time for all concerned.

Ask yourself

Are my meetings generally a waste of time?

- *A purposeless executive*. Too many people are busy being busy without having clear objectives and plans for each day.

Ask yourself

Do I plan each day and know what my objectives are?

Idea 3 – Carry out a time audit on yourself

> **Ask yourself**
>
> When I look in the mirror, do I see my biggest time waster?

Keep a record (a daily time log) of where your time currently goes – break your day into fifteen-minute chunks for recording purposes. Do this for a week or so and review after each batch of three or four days.

Peter Drucker's view is that only when we can manage time can we manage anything. In managing time we first need to know how we use it now and then change what and when we do things. Your time audit will probably confirm the findings of an IBM research, which showed that the four activities that take up over 50% of the average executive's time are:

1 meetings;
2 reading and writing business materials;
3 telephoning; and
4 travelling.

Your time audit can identify these and others by using symbols ascribed to activities, for example:

M   Meetings (in committee form)
Mi   Meetings (in one-to-one interview form)
F   Finance and figure work
T   Telephone

Wr	Writing
Wd	Writing letters or dictation
T	Travelling
R&D	Research and development
AOB	Any other business activity (should be specified)

Your time log can then be summarised in the following format shown overleaf:

Research indicates that we make assumptions about where our time goes and *overestimate* time spent on telephone calls, correspondence, report writing and planning, but *underestimate* time spent in meetings and one-to-one discussions. Keeping a record will confirm how you really spend your time and enable you to change how you spend it.

Analyse and improve your use of time

What elements can you readily identify which you can immediately change? Experience shows that improvements lie in changing the way you handle: interruptions (in person or by telephone); meetings; travel; and incoming/outgoing mail. You can improve your use of time if you ensure that:

- your time is spent according to a clear idea of your priorities and main responsibilities;
- you isolate the unimportant and ruthlessly prune out unnecessary or unproductive activities;
- you combine any 'free' time (i.e. free from meetings or other people's demands) to create meaningful and useable time of your own;
- tasks are simplified where others would not be adversely affected; and
- you are not doing tasks which could be performed by others.

Activity	Time Spent (in hours)	% of time	Comment (How to save time from now on)

How do you value other people's time?

It is vital to develop not only a personal sense of time, but also a sense of the value of other people's time.

Ask yourself

How do I measure up as a manager or mismanager of other people's working capital of time?

For example you should not frequently interrupt other people's meetings or assume that your telephone call to them is a welcome interruption. Missing deadlines, keeping people waiting, talking at great length at meetings, all indicate that you view other people's time as not being precious.

Idea 4 – Identify long-term goals

Before you do anything else or can achieve anything else, it is necessary to define your organisation's purpose and the purpose of your job, i.e. to what end is your time being expended.

Then, long-term goals can be set, in terms of the results that the organisation wishes to achieve (and your role as part of those goals being achieved).

Defining *the purpose of your organisation* requires an answer to the basic question: why does this organisation exist? You should be able to write this business purpose down.

Defining *the purpose of your own job* requires an answer to the question: why does my job exist? Again, you should be able to write this purpose down.

Identifying long-term goals, the strategy of your business and your part in it, will result from pondering these questions:

Where ...
- are we now?
- do we want to be in three or five years' time?

What ...
- strengths and weaknesses do we have?

How ...
- can we improve?
- can we get to where we want to be?

These same questions can be applied to your personal life.

The answers to these questions will help you identify long-term goals. The longer the time frame the more fuzzy the goals become, so you should then reduce your field of vision to focus on tangible, attainable, definable and measurable goals, but not lose sight of the far ground.

You should reach a point where you can be clear about long-term aims/directions and medium, or short-term goals/objectives which will be met and which will be part of a plan to continue on the road of achieving your longer-term aspirations.

Examples of short and long-term goals would be:

- Short-term: we should complete the planning stage of the product by the end of next month.
- Medium-term: by the end of next year we should have five new products on the market.

- Long-term: within five years we want to be the leading European supplier of electrical light fittings.

Remind yourself

To do NOW that which will be the best use of your time and which will advance you towards any of your goals.

Idea 5 – Make medium-term plans

In fixing your medium-term plans, the best method is to list your key areas of responsibility (and how your performance will be measured), and then set objectives with *time* budgeted for each. Use this chart to work it all out.

The review of objective achievement (the measure of your performance) should be at the intervals you have budgeted for each (e.g. 3, 6 or 12 months).

Smarter objectives

As a test of your objective-setting skills, remember they need to be Smarter, to the power of two, i.e. Smarter[2]:

Specific   &   Strategic
Measurable   &   Meaningful
Agreed   &   Attainable
Realistic   &   Rewarding

	Key area of responsibility	Objectives for each area of responsibility	Time budgeted to achieve each objective	Review of objective achievements
1	a b c	a b c	a b c	a b c
2	a b c	a b c	a b c	a b c
3	a b c	a b c	a b c	a b c
4	a b c	a b c	a b c	a b c
5	a b c	a b c	a b c	a b c

Time-bounded	&	Teambuilding
Evaluated	&	Empowering
Reviewed	&	Rewarding

Part of all this is to set out clear ways in which time management can be improved in the short to medium term. A 'Time Norm' form can help here.

Task/activity/procedure	Time taken now	Target time

When measuring and assessing improvements you cannot lose sight of the cost and quality dimension. Time improvements should not compromise standards set for those elements. Real improvement comes from keeping all three at whatever is decided are the acceptable levels – *time, cost, quality*.

Being successful in making medium-term plans requires you to:

- know the context (the longer term) in which you operate and how the medium and longer-term goals are linked;
- be able to plan and implement activity;
- set clear objectives and review progress toward them on a regular basis; and

- be flexible and adaptable to change in order to stay on course to meet objectives (unless you have changed those, too!).

Idea 6 – The Adair urgency/importance matrix

In the matrix you can identify tasks to:

1 Do now.
2 Plan for (to use quality time).
3 Do quickly (not requiring quality time).
4 Do later or perhaps delegate.

This approach has also been called the *Four-D system*: Drop it, Delay it, Delegate it, or Do it.

You should shape your plan for the day by listing the various components, prioritising them and planning the time accordingly.

- Make your plan at the end of the previous day or at the start of each day (whichever best suits you) enabling you to assess any unfinished work, together with upcoming priorities.
- List the main elements (in relation to yesterday's, today's and the week's plans).
- Prioritise those main elements and identify tasks according to the matrix 1, 2, 3 and 4 above.
- Group items together (e.g. telephone calls, correspondence).
- Decide when you will do the top priority tasks and block time out to do them.
- Decide on remaining tasks (and share your plan with assistants/staff as relevant).

Your plan of action for the day should follow these rules:

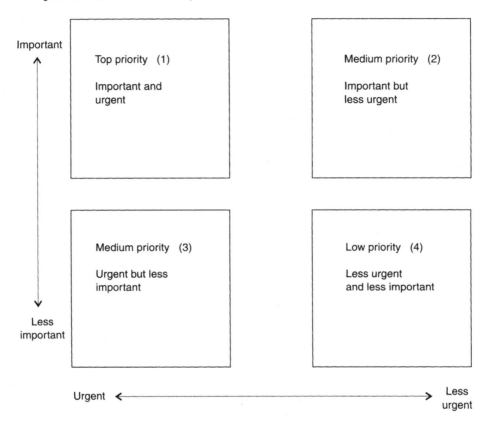

Important

Less important

Top priority   (1)

Important and urgent

Medium priority   (2)

Important but less urgent

Medium priority   (3)

Urgent but less important

Low priority   (4)

Less urgent and less important

Urgent   Less urgent

At a very basic level your list should also include your own system for identifying what must be done today, should be done today and what might be done today.

Think of any daily list as a kind of shopping list – how are you going to feel going home without an item being ticked off as done?

However, do not be fixed and inflexible, provided you have managed your time and time has not mismanaged you.

> ### Ask yourself
>
> Have I changed priorities deliberately? Do I need to get back on course and tackle what remain as being prioritised activities?

If you find your daily planning is not working well you should ask yourself first 'Am I at least achieving my highest priorities?'. If you are not, then you should review whether you are trying to accomplish too much in a day, not defining the task clearly enough, not planning what to do and when well enough, or finding it difficult to make decisions.

You might find that you are being 'blown of course' by interruptions, or doing things for other people. You should learn when to say 'no' and when to ensure your time is spent achieving your objectives if they are the most important.

> ### Management mantra
>
> I will concentrate more on doing the right thing and less on doing things right.

Idea 7 – Delegate efficiently

Select the type of work for delegation and consider to whom it can best be delegated.

Type of work	Delegation to enact
1 Technical/specialist work.	
a	a
b	b
c	c
2 Administrative/minor decisions.	
a	a
b	b
c	c
3 Where others are more qualified.	
a	a
b	b
c	c
4 Where staff development would result.	
a	a
b	b
c	c

The seven main reasons why CEOs do not delegate were revealed by research in five European countries to be:

1 It is risky.
2 We enjoy doing things.
3 We dare not sit and think.
4 It is a slow process.
5 We like to be 'on top of everything'.
6 Will our subordinates outstrip us?
7 'Nobody can do it as well as I can.'

So, what qualities must you have to be a good delegator?

There are five main tips:

1 Choose the right staff.
2 Train them.
3 Take care in briefing them, and ensuring their understanding of the 'why' and 'how to' of tasks delegated to them (and in imparting to them an understanding of business aims and policies).
4 Try not to interfere – stand back and support.
5 Control in a sensible and sensitive manner by checking progress at agreed intervals.

Checklist to test if you are an effective delegator

• Do you take work home evenings/weekends and/or work more than nine hours a day?
• Can you identify areas of work that you could/should delegate, but have not already done so?
• Do you define clearly the delegated tasks and satisfy yourself that the individual to whom they are delegated understands what is expected as an outcome?
• Can you trust people, or do you find it difficult to do so?
• Do you delegate authority and task?
• Do you think the delegated task will not be done as well by anyone else?
• Do you involve those to whom tasks have been delegated in the whole planning and problem-solving process?

> **Management mantra**
>
> You will never have so much authority as when you begin to give it away.

Idea 8 – Make use of committed time

You can increase your achievement level by using committed time (time that is 'booked' – for example travelling, meal-times) by: in the case of travelling time, ensuring that you use it to carry out, for example, reading, writing, thinking, having meetings, making phone calls, listening to 'improvement' tapes; in the case of meal times, ensuring that you use them, where relevant, to hold business conversations or meetings.

In other words, you should establish productive activities to schedule alongside time which has to be committed to other activities, e.g.:

- Daily routines: use dressing, bath-time/meals etc. by stimulating your mind e.g. with an improving tape.
- Waiting time: do not waste it – read or make phone calls.
- Travel time: use it productively – reading, planning, making phone calls or listening to tapes.
- Television: do not let it consume too much of every evening – do something productive for yourself and your personal goals.

Idea 9 – Manage your health and avoid stress

Time management has to be as much about ensuring that you maximise the amount of time you have available to use, as well as using the time wisely. That means taking steps to ensure you do not suffer time deprivation through illness of mind or body.

It is vital to look after your energy levels – to top up your batteries regularly – to discharge efficiently in a long-life fashion.

How topped-up are your batteries?

This is a five point test:

1   Sleep – are you getting enough? (Guide – eight hours or slightly less with age.)
2   Holidays – do you take and enjoy your full entitlement?
3   Thinking time – do you think about what you are doing in life and in work, even for a few minutes each day?
4   Exercise – honestly, what are you doing each week? (Guide – three sessions of 20 minutes per week – even brisk walks – is a reasonable aim.)
5   Eating habits – are you being sensible? (Guide – moderation in all things.)

Stress

Time and stress are cyclists on the same tandem. Bad management of one pushes the other out of control.

You should always watch out for signs of stress in yourself and others and take corrective action.

Warning bells should sound if any of the following are present in behavioural patterns:

1   Irritability.
2   Ever-present anxiety/worry.
3   Constant tiredness.
4   Increased consumption:
    • alcohol;
    • cigarettes; or
    • drugs.
5   Over-eating or the loss of appetite.
6   Memory lapses.
7   Loss of a sense of humour.
8   Feelings of nausea/fainting spells.
9   Poor sleep patterns.
10 Nail-biting, nervous mannerisms/'tics'.
11 Feelings of tension and headaches.
12 Indigestion.
13 Loss of concentration.
14 Unable to relax.
15 Feeling unable to cope.
16 Indecision.
17 Erratic driving.
18 Dependence on sleeping pills.
19 Sweating for no apparent reason.
20 Frequently crying or wanting to cry.

Research (in ten countries on a thousand managers) reveals that improving time management can help eliminate the 12 most common roots of stress in managers, which are:

1   Time pressures and deadlines.
2   Work overload.
3   Inadequately trained subordinates.

4   Long working hours.
5   Attending meetings.
6   Demands of work on private and social life.
7   Keeping up with new technology.
8   Holding beliefs conflicting with those of the organisation.
9   Taking work home.
10   Lack of power and influence.
11   The amount of travel required by work.
12   Doing a job below one's level of competence.

If you find yourself suffering from stress then you must:

1   Do something about it: look at the stress factors and assess what can be done to change your life at work/home.
2   Express yourself: talk to people about how you are feeling and the concerns you have (even directly to a person who might be causing part of your stress).
3   Evaluate priorities: check the balance of your life, take stock of activities and priorities and change them if necessary.
4   Accept what you cannot control: have the courage to change the things that can be changed, the serenity to accept the things that cannot be changed and the wisdom to know the difference.
5   Use your negative experience to positively change your behaviour.
6   Use time management skills to take charge of your time and how it is spent, particularly making time to deal with stress-causing problems. Get them out of the way.
7   Count your blessings – list those things that you are pleased with, about yourself or your achievements. Do not over concentrate on the past (guilt) or the future (anxiety).

8 Ask yourself – what is the worst that can happen and can I cope with that? Use this to reduce anxiety about an issue.

Ask yourself

How many of the 20 stress-related behaviours have I exhibited over the last 12 months? How many of the 12 roots of stress relate to me? What am I going to do about it – starting now?

Five Greatest Ideas for Organising your Office Work

Idea 10 – How to deal with interruptions – five techniques to keep them brief

- Meet people in *their* office whenever you can (you control your leaving time).
- Stand rather than sit for casual visitors (this controls the length of their stay).
- Keep a focus on time (mention the time you have available, refer to your next meeting and have a visible and watched clock).
- Stick to the point and avoid butterflying from main topic to unrelated ones.
- Be firm in a pleasant way.

Idea 11 – How to deal with paperwork and save an hour of time every day

- Do you see only what you should?
- Do you keep your desk clear of extraneous paperwork?
- Do you handle each piece of paper only once? (This one idea is known to save up to one hour per day or 220 hours a year!)
- Do you prioritise your paperwork (into action, information, reading, or for the waste bin)?
- Do you limit the amount of paperwork you generate for others?
- Can you pick out salient points quickly and know when to skip read or read in-depth?

Idea 12 – Five organising ideas to improve time management

1 Arrange your office or office space for ease of work, comfort and efficiency. Few people give this any thought at all.
2 Operate a clear desk policy – concentration is helped by doing one thing at a time so your desk should only have on it, the specific job that you are tackling at the time
3 Write effectively, keeping it short and simple by thinking of the main point first and ordering your thoughts for logical expression.
4 Telephone – keep a log to see how time efficient you are now! Then get used to planning for each call you make (the salient points you want to make); grouping incoming and outgoing calls (usually for the end of the day when people are less verbose); and use a timer (e.g. an egg timer – to keep all calls to a maximum of four minutes). Do not be afraid to put a block on incoming calls to reduce interruptions.
5 If you have an assistant, use him or her to deal with or to redirect (helpfully) any mail or callers (whether in person or on the telephone), where he/she or someone else could better deal with them. Strive for excellence not perfection, through your assistant.

Idea 13 – How to manage meetings

Your approach to meetings should be to confront three main issues:

- Is the meeting strictly necessary at all?
- How much time (particularly mine) is it worth?
- Will it run to time?

You must always have a clear idea of how much a meeting costs (in people's time, including your own) and whether it is worth it in results.

These are the hallmarks of successfully managed meetings:

- Meetings are planned ahead (who should attend; and with the agenda and any useful papers being circulated in advance).
- Times for each item and the meeting itself are set in advance (and adhered to).
- Minutes are concise and action-oriented (with responsibilities allocated).
- There is clarity of outcomes (shared by all).
- Meetings are reviewed constantly for effectiveness.
- The focus is on the positive.
- You are a successful umpire and referee.

Ask yourself

Is this meeting really necessary?

Idea 14 – Recognise the Adair five types of meeting

Before holding any meeting, ask yourself these five questions:

1 Why are we meeting?
2 What would be the result of not having the meeting, or what should result from having it?
3 Who should attend?
4 How long should it be and how should it be structured?
5 When is the best time to hold it?

You cannot ban all meetings, so you must manage them to get the best results. To do this you need to identify the type of meeting as follows.

The Adair five types of meeting

1 Briefing meetings – to impart and share information, to clarify points and incorporate ideas from others.
2 Advisory meetings – to gather views and advice and to outline or share any ideas.
3 'Council' meetings – to make and share responsibility for decisions, resolving differences on the way.
4 Committee meetings – to 'vote' decisions and reach compromises/accommodations of different views on matters of common concern.
5 Negotiating meetings – to reach decisions by bargaining with other parties who are acting in their own best interest.

You should decide what each type of meeting you are to be involved with actually is and plan to run each type as time efficiently as possible depending on their purpose.

Having decided that a meeting is really necessary, you should consider how much of your time (and other people's) the subject of it is worth. It should then begin and end on time. You should manage a meeting to ensure that progress is made and action decided. It is vital to get the involvement of all present (or else why are they there) and end on a positive note.

Being aware of the cost of meetings will focus the mind and planning will focus your actions. Minutes to record actions agreed and responsibilities should be in a form to give ease of follow-up and subsequent checking.

Summary and follow-up test

Keep the Adair ten principles of time management in the forefront of your mind and in your planning and prioritising.

The Adair ten principles of time management

1 Develop a personal sense of time.
2 Identify long-term goals.
3 Make medium-term plans.
4 Plan the day.
5 Make the best use of your best time.
6 Organise office work.
7 Manage meetings.
8 Delegate effectively.
9 Make use of committed time.
10 Manage your health.

Follow-up test

You should periodically test your time management and organising skills by asking yourself these questions:

1 Do I know where my time goes?
2 Can I handle interruptions effectively?
3 Do I have problems in chairing meetings?
4 Do I have a system for dealing with paperwork?
5 Do I always plan the day and prioritise the tasks to be done?

6 Have I defined 'purpose' in my personal and business life?
7 Have I identified long-term goals?
8 Have I set goals and objectives?
9 Have I made short, medium and long-terms plans?
10 Have I budgeted *time* to achieve goals/objectives?

Management mantra

Perfection may elude me, but I can achieve excellence.

Part Two

Understanding Leadership

Introduction

John Adair's greatest leadership ideas are enshrined in his fundamental analysis, the three circles, essentially the 'Task: Team: Individual' elements. As an effective leader or manager, you will need to keep this trinity of concepts sacred and think 'Task: Team: Individual' at all times. This section of the book examines the key ideas in understanding the functions of leadership.

Managers at all levels are business leaders. The business (literally the area in which one is busy) is about producing quality products or services at a profit (or at least in the most cost-effective way). At the heart of that role lie the three overlapping core responsibilities of any leader.

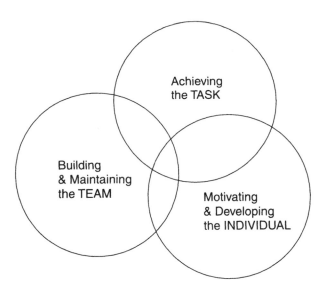

Achieving the *task*, building and maintaining the *team* and motivating and developing the *individual*.

This model implies an understanding of the environment in which one is working, as well as the need to possess or develop the necessary qualities of personality, character and skills to provide the necessary leadership functions – defining the objective, planning, briefing, controlling, informing, supporting and reviewing.

The three circles of leadership functions integrate together what we customarily call leadership and management, but these concepts do retain distinct overtones:

- *Leading* is about: giving direction, especially in times of change; inspiring or motivating people to work willingly; building and maintaining teamwork; providing an example; producing a personal output.
- *Managing* is about: running the business in 'steady state' conditions; day-to-day administration; organising structures and establishing systems; controlling, especially by financial methods.

Both sets of skills and activities are essential. You have to be a manager-leader or leader-manager depending on your specific role and/or level of responsibility in the organisation.

Management mantra

Management is prose, leadership is poetry.

Five Greatest Ideas for Understanding the Functions of Leadership

Idea 15 – Task, team and individual

In leadership, there are always three elements or variables:

1 The leader: qualities of personality and character.
2 The situation: partly constant, partly varying.
3 The group: the followers: their needs and values.

It is helpful to look at leadership functions in relation to the needs of work groups. These needs can be seen as three overlapping needs:

1 Task need: to achieve the common task.
2 Team maintenance needs: to be held together or to maintain themselves as a team.
3 Individual needs: the needs which individuals bring with them into the group.

These three needs (the task, team and individual) are the watchwords of leadership and people expect their leaders to:

- help them achieve the common task;
- build the synergy of teamwork; and
- respond to individuals and meet their needs.

The *task* needs work groups or organisations to come into being because the task needs doing and cannot be done by one person alone. The task has needs because pressure is built up to accomplish it to avoid frustration in the people involved if they are prevented from completing it.

The *team maintenance* needs are present because the creation, promotion and retention of group/organisational cohesiveness is essential on the 'united we stand, divided we fall' principle.

The *individual* needs are the physical ones (e.g. salary) and the psychological ones of:

- recognition;
- a sense of doing something worthwhile;
- status; and
- the deeper need to give and to receive from other people in a working situation.

The Task, Team and Individual needs overlap. This overlapping is evident in that:

- achieving the task builds the team and satisfies the individuals;
- if team maintenance fails (the team lacks cohesiveness) performance on the task is impaired and individual satisfaction is reduced; and
- if individual needs are not met, the team will lack cohesiveness and performance of the task will be impaired.

Ask yourself

When approaching business problems, issues or situations, do I always think: Task, Team and Individual?

Idea 16 – Leadership function – action-centred leadership

At whatever level of leadership, Task, Team and Individual *needs* must be constantly thought about. To achieve the common task, maintain teamwork and satisfy the individuals, certain functions have to be performed. A *function* is what leaders *do* as opposed to a *quality*, which is an aspect of what they *are*.

These functions (the *functional approach* to leadership, also called *action-centred leadership*) are:

- defining the task;
- planning;
- briefing;
- controlling;
- evaluating;

- motivating;
- organising; and
- providing an example.

Leadership functions in relation to Task, Team and Individual can be represented by the diagram below.

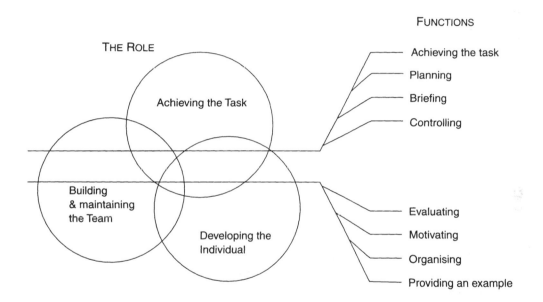

These leadership functions need to be handled with excellence and this is achieved by performing those functions with increasing skill.

Before examining the skills of leadership, it is worth seeing where certain qualities of leadership can be viewed as having functional value. These can be examined as leadership characteristics.

Idea 17 – Leadership characteristics – task element

Before you can start to develop skills in leadership, identify certain key *qualities* and typical outcomes that they achieve in managing *tasks*.

The need	Quality	Functional value
Task	Initiative	Gets the group moving
	Perseverance	Prevents the group giving up
	Efficiency	Work done well knowing costs (energy, time and money)
	Honesty	Establishing facts
	Self-confidence	Facing facts
	Industry	Steady application pays dividends
	Audacity	When not to be restrained by rules or convention
	Humility	Facing up to mistakes and not blaming others

Ask yourself

How many of these qualities do I possess? How can I develop those I don't and improve those I do?

Idea 18 - Leadership characteristics - team element

The key qualities needed to build and run a *team* successfully are these:

The need	Quality	Functional value
Team	Integrity	Integrating the team and creating trust
	Humour	Relieving tension and maintaining a sense of proportion
	Audacity	Inspire through originality or verve
	Self-confidence	Trusted by others
	Justice	Fair dealing builds group discipline
	Honesty	Wins respect
	Humility	Not selfish, shares praise, not arrogant and divisive

---

Ask yourself

When was the last time you laughed with a colleague in the office? Do you take yourself too seriously?

Management mantra

United we stand, divided we fall.

Idea 19 – Leadership characteristics – individual element

Dealing successfully with individuals is very different from dealing with your team. *Justice* is common to both. Somehow you've got to balance qualities of self-confidence and audacity with those of compassion and humility if you're to do the job really well.

The need	Quality	Functional value
Individual	Tact	Sensitive in dealing with people
	Compassion	Sympathetic awareness and help
	Consistency	People know where they stand
	Humility	Recognises qualities/abilities and gives credit
	Honesty	Wins individual respect
	Justice	Fair dealing encourages individuals

Remind yourself

Whilst the whole may be greater than the sum of the parts, the whole is made up of parts – each individual contribution counts.

Summary and follow-up test

Leadership centres on:

- the leader – qualities of personality and character;
- the situation – partly constant, partly varying;

- the team – the followers: their needs and values; and
- the overlapping needs of the Task, Team and Individual.

Leadership functions can be summarised as:

- defining the task;
- planning;
- briefing;
- controlling;
- evaluating;
- motivating;
- organising; and
- providing an example.

Follow-up test

- Have you challenged your leadership strengths/weaknesses and addressed your development needs?
- Have you continuously addressed the functions of leadership?
- Do you constantly focus on Task, Team and Individual?

Management mantra

Leadership is action not position.

Part Three

Performing As A Leader

Introduction

The greatest ideas for performing as a leader are grouped under the key areas of: setting and achieving objectives, making decisions, developing leadership skills and team-building.

Three Greatest Ideas for Setting and Achieving your Objectives

Idea 20 – Draw up a personal profile

The starting point is to self-assess and take stock of yourself in the overall context of the direction you would like to be heading.

Personal profile

1 What are my strengths/what special skills do I have?
2 What are my values (i.e. what is important and worthwhile to me)?
3 What would be my preferred ways of earning a living?
4 What activities/situations do I want to avoid?
5 What achievements would I like to list as having been successfully met in my life?
6 What would I like the highlights of my obituary to be? (This is a really good way of focusing the mind, as is asking yourself how you would like your epitaph to read.)

Ask yourself

Do I regularly take stock of my skills, values and preferences?

Idea 21 – Set personal goals

Answering the above questions in 20, will enable you to set out more clearly the goals/objectives you want to achieve in your life and, linked with your time management skills, to plan the important steps to take to achieve them. You will then be able to 'add years to your life and more life to your years'.

Again the approach is to work from the long term back to the short term as in:

1   What are my lifetime goals/objectives?
2   What are my five-year goals/objectives?
3   What goals/objectives will I set for achievement within one year?

Taking this approach will ensure that you concentrate on those goals/objectives which are important to you. The strategic element of your approach will then ensure that you analyse the obstacles that have to be overcome and plan your priorities and the ways/means to achieve your one-year, five-year and lifetime goals/objectives.

Ask yourself

For each set of goals/objectives:

1 Have I identified obstacles and opportunities?
2 What are the ways/means to achieve goals/objectives, despite/because of those obstacles/opportunities?

This will give you your plan(s) of how to achieve your personal goals/objectives, which you must then implement!

Remind yourself

Set goals and measure progress towards them and be prepared to review the goals themselves for continuing relevance.

Idea 22 – Set professional business goals

As has been seen, your strategic aims result from asking the questions:

- Where are we now?
- Where do we want to be in three or five years' time?
- What strengths and weaknesses do we have?
- How can we improve?
- Can we get to where we want to be?

As for setting personal goals/objectives, your professional business goals/objectives (for your organisation and, perhaps separately, for yourself at work), should be delineated:

1   What are the key long-term goals/objectives?
2   What are the five-year goals/objectives?
3   What are the one-year goals/objectives?

Then, plans/strategies have to be addressed as in:

1   Identifying obstacles and opportunities.
2   Analysing ways/means to achieve goals/objectives despite/because of those obstacles/opportunities.

Planning answers the question: *How are we going to achieve* a particular task, meet a goal or reach an objective? How leads to who, what and when? You can then set out your strategy for achieving:

- short-term goals/objectives – the one year;
- medium-term goals/objectives – the five years; and
- long-term goals/objectives.

Goals/objectives must be clear, specific, measurable, attainable, written, time-bounded, realistic, challenging, agreed, consistent, worthwhile, and participative.

Attaining goals/objectives brings into play strategy and planning, for which you need imagination, a sense of reality, power of analysis and what has been described as helicopter vision (the ability to see matters in detail, but from a higher perspective).

An operational plan/strategy should contain:

- a *smarter*[2] set of goals/objectives; and
- plans/stratagems for achieving them.

The plan should detail all the steps required to complete those tasks that are needed to be done in order to meet the objectives set.

Time spent on planning is crucial in the thinking, the brainstorming and the sharing of ideas, the definition of purpose, the identification of obstacles and the ways and means of overcoming them and of meeting objectives.

It is necessary, of course, to get the right balance between planning and implementation. Planning saves time at the strategic and operational level and the key principle is every moment spent planning saves three or four in execution.

Management mantra

If you do not know where you are going, you can take any road.

*T*welve *G*reatest *I*deas for Decision-*M*aking

Idea 23 – Refine your decision-making skills

You need to be able to choose the action or course of action that is the best for you/your organisation to meet its objective(s). An effective decision is one that produces the goods, i.e. gives the desired end result.

It is important to be able to project ahead, to take the expected and unexpected into account, to have contingency plans in case events intrude in such a way as will turn a good decision into a bad one.

There are usually several different decisions that can be taken and pressure to decide. Decide you must, even if trial and error is then used to assess the decision, amend it or overturn it.

Fear of failure must not serve to make you risk-averse, rather it should push you harder to 'think until it hurts'.

The effective decision has these six elements:

1 Defining the objective.
2 Gathering sufficient information.
3 Identifying the feasible options.
4 Evaluating those options.
5 Making the decision (choosing an option).
6 Testing its implementation: by feel, by measurement and by assessment.

You should also listen to your 'feel-right?' test – do warning lights flash or alarm bells sound? If so, re-work decision elements 1–6. (Experience of your own or that of others helps to develop your 'feel' for decisions.)

A decision is only effective if it is implemented (and that means getting the desired results through people). For that, other people need to be included in the decision-making process. You need to develop your skills in appreciating when it is most appropriate to include others in the decision-making process.

Idea 24 – The decision-maker as effective thinker

An effective decision-maker is always an effective thinker. The three essential skills are those of:

- analysing;
- synthesising; and
- valuing.

An effective decision-maker knows that quick decisions are not necessarily the best ones and decisiveness only results from thinking things through. Key decisions (and recognising when you are being asked to make or be involved in the making of key decisions) demand that great care must go into analysing (the component elements), synthesising (putting ideas together) and valuing (assessing relative worth).

The crucial elements in decision-making are:

- establish the facts;
- consider the options; and
- decide the course of action.

The truly effective thinker has these attributes:

1 Skills of analysis, synthesis and valuing.
2 Open to intuition.
3 Imagination (to find new ways to overcome problems).
4 Creativity (coupled with careful preliminary work).
5 Open to new ideas.
6 Humility – when to recognise that others may have better powers or knowledge and to combine with their thinking.

Two maxims are useful in decision-making:

1 'It can be done.'
2 'Always try to turn a disadvantage into an advantage.'

Management mantra

This problem is an opportunity in disguise.

Always operate in the context of facing reality and of seeking and speaking the truth.

To improve your performance you need to ask yourself how good your skills are (and have been) at:

- decision-making;
- problem-solving; and
- creative thinking.

> **Ask yourself**
>
> Do I make false assumptions and jump to conclusions? Am I prone to faulty reasoning or of not listening to others?

Idea 25 – The manager as decision-maker

> **Remind yourself**
>
> Management is 'deciding what to do and getting it done'.

Success in business stems from good quality management decisions first of all and then the effectiveness in implementation which depends on the skills of leadership, influencing, communication and motivation.

One survey (of 200 leaders of industry and commerce) ranked 'the ability to take decisions' as the most important attribute of top management.

The logical or rational manager will invariably follow this decision-making model: define objective; collect information; develop options; evaluate and decide; implement; monitor consequences; and sense effects.

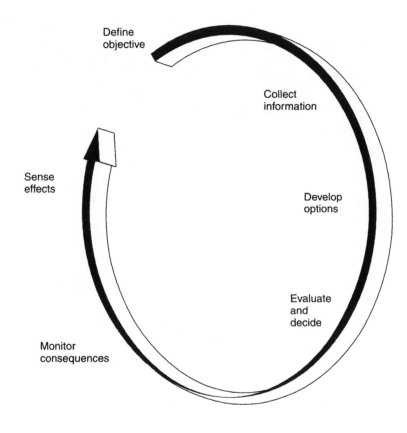

Define
objective

Collect
information

Develop
options

Evaluate
and
decide

Implement

Monitor
consequences

Sense
effects

Idea 26 – How to avoid the trap of compromise decisions

US research into decisions by public sector officials suggests that decision-makers rarely settle for the 'best' or optimum solution, being affected by emotion, power politics, the influences of other people and by their own values. Often a decision is a compromise between different courses of action, being one that:

- agrees to some extent with one's own personal interests, needs or values;
- meets the value standards of superiors;
- is acceptable to those affected (by the decision and for carrying it out);
- looks reasonable; and
- has an escape element of self-justification if it all goes wrong.

Clearly such approaches to decision-making must be removed from your approach!

Idea 27 – How to use analysis in decision-making

An essential ability in analysing is to be able to break the whole up into its component parts, particularly complex matters into its simple elements.

The hallmarks of the analytical mind are that it:

1 establishes the relationship between the parts and the whole;
2 finds the root cause(s) of the problem; and
3 identifies the issue(s) at stake, the 'either/or' upon which a decision rests.

Analytical ability is improved by:

- working from first principles;
- establishing the facts and separating them from opinions, assumptions or suppositions;
- asking yourself questions (as in 'When did the problem first arise?' as well as our six friends Who, What, Why, When, Where and How?);
- constantly checking the premise and/or logical steps which can undermine good reasoning;
- thinking backwards from the desired outcome;
- organising the facts; and
- seeing the problem as a solution in disguise.

Analysis is not, however, an end in itself and trying to over-analyse can lead to inactivity or 'paralysis by analysis' as it has been called.

Idea 28 – The role of synthesis – a holistic approach – in decision-making

Decision-making requires an individual to 'take a view' and that depends on the ability to combine parts or elements to form a whole: synthesis. Holistic is a useful word to use in this regard as it also conveys the approach, especially in business, which recognises that 'wholes' are produced by grouping various units together; where it is difficult to analyse them in their parts without losing this wholeness. Hence a holistic view needs to be taken in business decision-making.

One difficulty is that analysis can be the enemy of synthesis (holism) and vice versa. There is a need in business to be able to see the wood for the trees (holism) rather than only the trees (analysis).

In this sense, and in business too, the whole is greater than the sum of its parts. Business thinking is a good example of the Gestalt approach whereby we arrive at an understanding of:

- the overall significance rather than a mechanistic explanation; and
- the relationships between events not just the events themselves which do not occur in isolation, only in a setting which gives each significance.

Managers need to take this whole view – not to see things as a marketing problem, or a production issue, or a stock control difficulty, or a people problem, or a management failure. Look at the whole to see what that can yield by way of a solution.

Integration of facts, ideas and opinions is like the ability to synthesise, and strengthens the manager's decision-making. Particularly in assessing financial performance, a manager needs to view the figures as a whole as well as in detail.

Idea 29 – The role of imagination in decision-making

This is an important attribute to have in business: the skill to visualise the whole in one's imagination. It is part and parcel of being creative in the approach to decision-making. Being imaginative is a crucial ability to develop in oneself and others: it helps to surprise the competition, to exploit the unexpected, to invent new products or services, or to solve problems creatively. Indicators of a healthy level of imagination are the abilities to:

- recall events easily and visually;
- foresee what may happen before an event;
- be inventive or creative artistically, mechanically or verbally; and
- fantasise about future events.

These elements of recall, visualising, creating, foreseeing and fantasising contribute to effective thinking in business as much as in the arts or scientific fields.

Idea 30 – The role of conceptual thinking in decision-making

Although a concept may appear to be an abstraction arrived at by analysis, it has a different feel because:

- it is a whole (and as such more than the sum of its parts); and
- it is a developing entity in its own right.

A concept is 'something conceived in the mind' and conceptual thinking in business addresses such issues as:

- What business are we in?
- What are its strengths/weaknesses?
- What are its purposes/aims?

Conceptual thinking should be kept separate from decision-making, even though decisions are made on the basis of the concepts that we have.

Concepts can be used in 'profiling' business development, but they then have to be made more specific in the form of proposals or plans, before being implemented. Concepts can be a way of taking your mind away from the particular and include the ideas of what ought to be as opposed to what is. Good quality concepts will underpin good quality business decisions. Therefore you should generate clear, well-defined concepts and develop them.

Idea 31 – The role of intuition in decision-making

Being intuitive, successfully so, is undoubtedly a help in making effective decisions. It is not always possible to analyse problems into solutions, and intuition is the useful power to know what has happened or what to do. Interestingly the powers of intuition are diminished by stress and general fatigue and so your ability to be insightful in decision-making can be adversely affected by these factors.

'Intuition', 'instinct', 'first impressions', 'feel', 'hunch' and 'flair' are important dimensions to explore when faced not only with decision-making, but also considering business activities and the systems to run them.

It is too easy to be dismissive of intuition, of being able to 'sense' what needs to be done or to 'smell' trouble/opportunities. On the contrary, it is an invaluable key to making and taking effective decisions.

Idea 32 – The role of originality and innovation in decision-making

Creative and innovative thinking can help in making decisions that develop a business so they are elements to encourage in yourself and others. Be prepared to work at problems/issues to encourage creativity or insight coming into play and be prepared to encourage new ideas (by rewarding those who put them forward), to try out and innovate new products/services as well as new ways of doing things.

Idea 33 – The concept of value in decision-making

Along with analysis and synthesis, valuing is the third essential in effective thinking and decision-making. The ability to make decisions has two main aspects:

1 to establish the truth or true facts; and
2 to know what to do.

Time must be taken on the first, otherwise integrity, or the value of truth, is lost in the process. Thinking first and then deciding what to do is the correct order in decision-making. Getting at the truth should make knowing what to do easier.

In many respects, it is better to behave as if truth is an object, that it must be discovered. The truth, and valuing what one discovers, should be seen as 'objective' with one's own views and conditioning recognised and relied on or discounted as needs be.

When you rely on others, as managers so often do, you may have to sift information from their 'valuations' (information plus judgement). This is another form of valuing – of knowing who and when to trust to give you truth, or truth backed by acceptable value judgements. Questioning is a valid part of establishing the credentials of the adviser and the credibility of the advice. Can you trust the person to tell the truth backed by sufficient expertise or insight? You will learn by experience to recognise the people who:

- tell you what they think you want to hear;
- express a view thinking it might agree with your own;
- are watching their backs; or
- try to hide things.

Be scrupulous in establishing the truth – ask questions until you are satisfied you have it right.

You are good at valuing if you can say that invariably you have good judgement and the converse is also true. Knowing the truth or reality can then be followed by deciding what to do.

Also, beware of inaccurate figures (even from accounts departments!), errors in facts, figures and assumptions and specious assurances – all must be tested for accuracy and 'truth'.

Idea 34 – How to weigh up the options in decision-making

It is invariably necessary to choose a particular course of action out of a range of possible 'options'. What is the best way of ensuring that your own selection process is a sound one? The basic point here is that you should never assume that there is only one option open to you. Consider a number of options (or as many sensible and pertinent ones as you can muster), many of which will be directly dictated or affected by the facts that you can establish. Gathering information also helps the collection of options, even considering options that you might think are closed to you (e.g. increasing price, scrapping low-profit items etc.).

Selecting and working through a range of options means considering:

- Which are the possible ones?
- Which of those are feasible?
- How to reduce feasible options to two choices, the 'either/or'?
- Which one to choose (or a mixture)?
- Whether any action is really necessary at all, now, later?
- Whether or not to keep options open, i.e. not to choose yet?

You should avoid any compulsion to take action through an option where no action would be better and you should avoid assuming that there are only two possibilities, until you have weighed up all the feasible ones you can in a reasonable time frame.

Whilst considering the options beware false assumptions: test all for validity.

At the same time, it is essential to understand the other factors that can limit the range and choice of options or their applicability. Judgement (again beware false assumptions – including about these factors) is needed about:

1   time;
2   information;
3   resources; and
4   knowledge.

You have to know the real (not assumed) limits, which the above factors can impose on the options available to you.

Generating options, particularly if, initially, there seems to be only one, will usually lead to better decision-making. This is where imagination, creative thinking and intuition can help.

Considering fresh possibilities and suspending judgement whilst generating them (through brainstorming) can increase the range of options by avoiding negativity as in:

- 'It won't work.'
- 'We do it this way.'
- 'It can't be done.'
- 'It failed before.'

In weighing the options you must refine your skills at considering the consequences, both the possible and the probable. This will lead to assessment of risk and reward and both should be carefully calculated.

Ask yourself

Can I accept the risk of failure? What is the worst that can happen if it fails, and can I accept it?

Judgement then is used in selecting from the range of options that have been carefully weighed and assessed as to their probable outcomes.

Remind yourself

When facing a difficult decision, it could be worth getting people together, asking for ideas or brainstorming them and testing and evaluating the suggestions.

Nine Greatest Ideas for Leadership Skills

The eight functions of leadership are: defining the task, planning, briefing, controlling, evaluating, motivating, organising, and setting an example. This section ends with the Adair Short Course on Leadership, which is especially useful in carrying out the briefing function of leadership.

Ask yourself

Am I a born leader, yet?

Idea 35 – Leadership skills – defining the task

A task is something that needs to be done. People in organisations and teams need to have this distilled into an objective, which is:

- clear;
- concrete;
- time-limited;
- realistic;

- challenging; and
- capable of evaluation.

Remind yourself

This is not MY task, it is OUR task – we share it because it has a value for the organisation and ourselves.

There are five tests to apply to the defining of a task and they are:

1   Do you have a clear idea of the objectives of your group now and for the next few years/months, which have been agreed with your boss?
2   Do you understand the overall aims and purpose of the organisation?
3   Can you set your group's objectives into the context of those larger intentions?
4   Is your present main objective specific, defined in terms of time and as concrete/tangible as you can make it?
5   Will the team know for itself if it succeeds or fails and does it get speedy feedback of results?

In defining the task/communicating the objective, you need to have the following abilities:

- To tell the group the objective you have been given.
  BEWARE: not understanding it yourself can lead to lack of clarity.
- To tell the group what to do and why.
  BEWARE: giving the reason in terms of a past event rather than future.
- To break down aims into objectives for other groups.

BEWARE: not making them specific enough or not making sure there are enough objectives which add up to complete the aim.

- To agree the objective.
  BEWARE: taking things for granted and not fixing on the objective.
- To relate the aim to the purpose (to answer what and why questions).
  BEWARE: confusing your division's aim with the purpose of the organisation.
- To define the purpose and check that the aims relate to it and to each other.
  BEWARE: not doing it often enough.
- To redefine the purpose to generalise it and create more aims and objectives.
  BEWARE: causing confusion by doing it too often, or not knowing that it has to be done.
- To communicate purpose to employees.
  BEWARE: using the wrong language, by-passing leaders below you, or relying on others doing it for you.

In defining the task, it needs to be broken down into objectives, aims and purpose so that it can be communicated with clarity. The end of the task should also be defined when the need arises and all should be aware of what the success criteria will be.

Idea 36 – Leadership skills – planning

This key activity for any team or organisation requires a search for alternatives and that is best done with others in an open-minded, encouraging and creative way. Foreseeable contingencies should always be planned for.

Management mantra

In SAS slang, the seven Ps are: Proper Planning and Preparation Prevents Piss Poor Performance.

Planning requires that the what, why, when, how, where and who questions are answered. Plans should be tested . . .

Checklist to test plans

- Have I called upon specialist advice?
- Have all feasible courses of action been considered and weighed up in terms of resources needed/available, and outcomes?
- Has a programme been established which will achieve the objective?
- Is there a provision for contingencies?
- Were more creative solutions searched for as a basis for the plan?
- Is the plan simple and as foolproof as possible, rather than complicated?
- Does the plan include necessary preparation or training of the team and its members?
- In ensuring that there is the appropriate level of participation in the planning process, the chart below may be useful.

The planning continuum

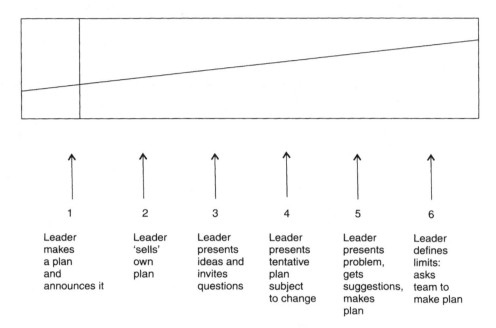

1	2	3	4	5	6
Leader makes a plan and announces it	Leader 'sells' own plan	Leader presents ideas and invites questions	Leader presents tentative plan subject to change	Leader presents problem, gets suggestions, makes plan	Leader defines limits: asks team to make plan

Idea 37 – Leadership skills – briefing

Briefing or instructing a team is a basic leadership function, usually conducted face-to-face. Any briefing is an opportunity to:

- create the right atmosphere;
- promote teamwork; and
- get to know, encourage and motivate each individual.

Before and after any briefing session, to ensure that the question of 'what is my role in all this?' (which will be on everyone's mind) is answered, you need to ask yourself these questions:

1 Does every individual know exactly what his/her job is?
2 Does each member of the team have clearly defined targets and performance standards agreed with me?
3 Does each person know at the end what is expected of him/her and how that contribution or that of his/her team fits in with the purposeful work of everyone else?

Communicating (speaking and listening) is crucial to get right in any briefing and it centres on the task, team and individual needs that should be addressed.

The effective speaking attributes of a successful briefing are to be:

- prepared;
- clear;
- simple;
- vivid; and
- natural.

Ask yourself

Can I speak in a way that can move the team to the desired action?

Assertiveness can be important. For example, to give the task direction and in explaining the role of the team/individual, especially in an initial briefing or where there is low morale.

Idea 38 – Leadership skills – controlling

Excellent leaders get maximum results with the minimum of resources.

To control others, leaders need to exhibit self-control (but remembering that anger/sadness can be legitimate responses if the circumstances warrant it and are themselves mechanisms for control). Leaders also need to have good control systems (simple and effective to monitor financial and task performance) and to have control of what others should and should not be doing in order to meet objectives. The success at directing, regulating, restraining or encouraging individual and team efforts on the task (and in meetings) are the criteria for testing a leader's effectiveness as a 'controller'.

A checklist for testing controlling skills

Do I maintain a balance between controlling too tightly or giving too much freedom to the team?

Am I able to co-ordinate work-in-progress, bringing together all the parts in proper relation with each other?

In technical work, do I ensure that team and individual needs are met?

Do meetings I chair run over time(s) allotted to topics?

Do I have proper budgets and ways of monitoring actual performance?

Do customers rate my organisation's control systems for:

- quality of product/service;
- delivery;
- costs; and
- safety?

Remind yourself

To steer between the two rocks of too much interference and lack of direction.

Idea 39 – Leadership skills – evaluating

Leaders need to be good at:

- assessing the *consequences*;
- evaluating team *performance*;
- appraising and training *individuals*; and
- judging *people*.

In assessing the consequences, leaders should be able to foresee the outcome of action (or inaction) in terms of the technical, the financial and the human, and to ask probing questions of the team in order to establish the likely consequences.

In evaluating team performance, perhaps through a de-briefing session after a particular project, the performance of the team as a whole in relation to the task can be examined:

- Has it been a success, a partial success or a failure?
- Can lessons be learnt?
- Can action be taken to improve performance?
- What feedback can be given to ensure improvement?

The evaluation of the team is helpful in trying to build it into a high-performance one where the hallmarks are:

- clear, realistic objectives;
- shared sense of purpose;
- best use of resources;
- atmosphere of openness;
- handling failure; and
- riding out the storms.

In appraising and training individuals, the following agenda can be used:

- past performance;
- future work to be done: targets, priorities, standards and strategies;
- matching perceptions of what can be expected by each party of the other in order to achieve a good working relationship; and
- improving skill, knowledge, and behaviour.

Some tips in handling appraisals:

- have all necessary data available;
- put the other person at ease;
- control pace and direction of the interview;
- listen, listen, listen;
- avoid destructive criticism (encourage self-criticism);
- review performance systematically;
- discuss future action;
- discuss potential/aspirations;
- identify training/development required; and

- avoid common pitfalls, such as:
  - dominating the conversation;
  - making promises unlikely to be kept;
  - expecting dramatic changes overnight; and
  - blaming those not present.

In judging people, leaders decide who should do what and this always affects outcomes and so is a crucial skill. Leaders should not have favourites because:

- it destroys team unity;
- the favourite is a personification of your judgement about people – if others do not agree with your judgement, your credibility suffers; and
- favourites advance by recognising the social and esteem needs of their bosses and by pandering to them – the boss can have his/her judgement impaired by this.

Judgement is improved by analysing impressions formed, discussing them with others and by making decisions about people more slowly and after deliberation.
     In evaluation, you need to ensure that:

- your decision-making judgement is good;
- you appraise people regularly and well;
- you are good at judging people; and
- you evaluate your own performance as much as those who work for you.

Ask yourself

Do I also apply the principle of evaluation to myself and my work?

Idea 40 – Leadership skills – motivating

There are six key principles for motivating others:

1 Be motivated yourself.
2 Select people who are highly motivated.
3 Set realistic and challenging targets.
4 Remember that progress motivates.
5 Provide fair rewards.
6 Give recognition.

Individuals are motivated by their requirements to satisfy a (Maslow's) hierarchy of needs:

- physiological – hunger, thirst, sleep;
- safety – security, protection from danger;
- social – belonging, acceptance, social life, friendship and love;
- esteem – self-respect, achievement, status, recognition; and
- self-actualisation – growth, accomplishment, personal development.

Each individual will be at a different stage/level up this hierarchy of needs and will need to be motivated accordingly.

Other than in financial terms, individuals are usually motivated if they can see that they will be given:

- achievement;
- recognition;
- job interest;
- responsibility; and
- advancement.

A good leader provides the right climate and the opportunities for these needs to be met on an individual basis and this is perhaps the most difficult of a leader's challenges.

Leaders must also inspire others. In 1987, James Kouzes and Barry Posner identified five characteristics of what they call exemplary leaders:

- *Leaders challenge the process*. Leaders search for opportunities. They experiment and take risks, constantly challenging other people to exceed their own limitations.
- *Leaders inspire a shared vision*. Leaders envision an enabling future and enlist people to join in that new direction.
- *Leaders enable others to act*. Leaders strengthen others and foster collaboration.
- *Leaders model the way*. Leaders set the example for people by their own leadership behaviour and they plan small wins to get the process moving.
- *Leaders encourage the heart*. Leaders regard and recognise individual contributions and they celebrate team successes.

Management mantra

In the words of John Buchan: 'The test of leadership in not to put greatness into humanity, but to elicit it, for the greatness is there already.'

Idea 41 – Leadership skills – organising

Good leaders are good at:

- organising themselves – their own work and particularly how they manage themselves, their time and how they delegate;

- organising the team – to build and maintain it to ensure that there is good, effective team-work; and
- organising the organisation – the structure and the systems/processes in which, and by which, people operate.

Leaders change things and organise for the achievement of results – leading change requires considerable powers and skills of leadership. In all aspects, leaders must organise with a purpose clearly in mind at all times.

Leaders should consider their organising skills by reference to the Task, Team and Individual as follows:

Task
- Is there a common purpose?
- Is it broken down into aims and objectives?
- How is it/are they communicated?

Team
- What are the teams/sub-teams?
- How do they contribute to the purpose?
- Do they relate together as a team?

Individual
- Do they have freedom and discretion?
- Are individual needs being met?

Here are some further questions to ask yourself in surveying your organisation:

- Do the Task/Team/Individual circles overlap sufficiently to provide and maintain high morale in the face of difficulties?
- How are tensions resolved and are there adequate systems/disciplinary procedures/dispute handling methods in place?

A checklist to test the organising function ability

You

- Can you organise your personal and business life in ways which would improve your effectiveness as a leader?
- Do you delegate sufficiently?
- Can you identify improvements in your time management?

Team

- Is the size and make-up correct?
- Should a sub-team be set up?
- Are opportunities/procedures in place to ensure participation in decision-making?
- Do you restructure and change individuals' jobs as appropriate?

Organisation

- Do you have a clear idea of its purpose and how the parts should work together to achieve it?
- Are effective systems in place for training/recruitment/dismissal?
- Do you carry out surveys into the size of teams, number of leadership levels, growth of unnecessary complexity, line and staff co-operation, and properly working communications systems?
- Are you good at administration, recognising the performance of administrators and ensuring that administrative systems facilitate excellent performance from teams/individuals?

Management mantra

Organising is getting right the relations of the whole and the parts.

The size of working teams/groups should be examined to assess the importance of these factors:

- *Task/technology* – complexity narrows the span of control, i.e. is the team too big to control/handle this aspect and does it mesh properly with other teams?
- *Communications* – especially with geographical/physical dispersement, are they good enough?
- *Motivation and autonomy* – is the training commensurate with any wishes to be self-sufficient?
- *Competence of leaders* – are large teams led by good enough leaders, what are the leader's other commitments and does he/she have good/specialist support?

Idea 42 – Leadership skills – setting an example

'Leadership is example.' To be successful, a good leader must 'walk the talk'. Employees take a fraction of the time to know a leader as he/she takes to get to know them. The example you are giving is quite simply you. Whether this is a good or a bad example depends on the leader.

An example is set in verbal and non-verbal ways and all aspects of a leader's words and deeds must be considered in the light of this.

If example is contagious, it is worth ensuring that a good one is set to encourage the qualities sought in others.

Some key questions for good leadership are:

- Task – do you lead from the front/by example?
- Team – do you develop your teams' standards through the power of example?
- Individual – do you view each individual as a leader in their own right?

Bad examples, particularly of hypocrisy, are noticed more than good, so care must be taken in all that a leader says and does.

Ask yourself

- Do I set a good example?
- Do I ask others to do what I would be unwilling to do myself?
- Do people comment on the good example I set in my work?
- Does my (bad) example conflict with what all are trying to do?
- Can I quote when I last deliberately set out to give a lead example?
- Do I mention the importance of example to team leaders who report to me?

Idea 43 – The Adair short course on leadership

1 The six most important words . . . 'I admit I made a mistake'.
2 The five most important words . . . 'I am proud of you'.

3   The four most important words . . . 'What is your opinion?'
4   The three most important words . . . 'If you please'.
5   The two most important words . . . 'Thank you'.
6   The one most important word . . . 'We'.
7   The last, most unimportant word . . . 'I'.

Five Greatest Ideas for Teambuilding

Idea 44 – Teambuilding – the functions of the leader

Teambuilding is part of the leadership 'holy' trinity of Task, Team and Individual.

One of the main results of good leadership is a good team (see diagram).

In 1985, ICI believed that the outcomes of effective leadership were that people will:

- have a clear sense of direction and work hard and effectively;
- have confidence in their ability to achieve specific challenging objectives;
- believe in and be identified with the organisation;
- hold together when the going is rough;
- have respect for and trust in managers; and
- adapt to the changing world.

Good leadership characteristics	Team outcomes
Enthusing	Team members are purposefully busy and have a basis to judge priorities
Lives values such as integrity	Gives a sense of excitement and achievement with people willing to take risks and higher work loads
Leads by example	Consistency in knowing leader's values
Generates good leaders from followers	Is trusted
Aware of own behaviour and environment	Aspire to leader's example
Intellect to meet job needs	Confidence in leadership
Aware of team and individual needs	The led start to lead [with leader less indispensable] being delegated to, coached and supported
Exhibits trust	Inspires confidence and perfomance
Represents the organisation to the team and vice versa	Confidence of contribution to aims and commitment to them

In achieving the task, building the team and developing the individual, whilst leadership style may differ, effective leadership (in ICI's findings and its development courses) emphasised that the leader must do the following:

- feel personally responsible for his/her human, financial and material resources;
- be active in setting direction and accepting the risks of leadership;
- be able to articulate direction and objectives clearly and keep his/her people in the picture;
- use the appropriate behaviour and methods to gain commitment for the achievement of specific objectives; and
- maintain high standards of personal performance and demand high standards of performance from others.

Leaders in teambuilding provide the functions of:

- planning;
- initiating;
- controlling;
- supporting;
- informing; and
- evaluating.

Remind yourself

If you give people respect and trust, some real responsibility, together with a degree of independence, they will reward you with their best.

Idea 45 – Achieving the task – with a team

You should address the following questions, and answer 'yes' or 'no' to each. For each question which you have answered with a 'no' (or in the case of 'Training' and 'Supervision' with an unsatisfactory outcome) define how you are going to put things right – and by when.

- *Purpose*. Am I clear what the task is?
- *Responsibilities*. Am I clear what mine are?
- *Objectives*. Have I agreed these with my superior, the person accountable for the group?
- *Programme*. Have I worked one out to reach objectives?
- *Working conditions*. Are these right for the job?
- *Resources*. Are these adequate (authority, money, materials)?
- *Targets*. Has each member clearly defined and agreed them?
- *Authority*. Is the line of authority clear (Accountability chart)?
- *Training*. Are there any gaps in the specialist skills or abilities of individuals in the group required for the task?
- *Priorities*. Have I planned the time?
- *Progress*. Do I check this regularly and evaluate?
- *Supervision*. In case of my absence who covers for me?
- *Example*. Do I set standards by my behaviour?

Idea 46 – Building the team

Answer the questions below honestly, 'yes' or 'no'. If the answer is 'no' to any question, work out what you need to do to put matters right – and set yourself an achievable time target within which to do it.

- *Objectives*. Does the team clearly understand and accept them?
- *Standards*. Do they know what standards of performance are expected?
- *Safety standards*. Do they know the consequences of infringement?
- *Size of team*. Is the size correct?
- *Team members*. Are the right people working together? Is there a need for sub-groups to be constituted?
- *Team spirit*. Do I look for opportunities for building teamwork into jobs? Do methods of pay and bonus help to develop team spirit?
- *Discipline*. Are the rules seen to be reasonable? Am I fair and impartial in enforcing them?
- *Grievances*. Are grievances dealt with promptly? Do I take action on matters likely to disrupt the group?
- *Consultation*. Is this genuine? Do I encourage and welcome ideas and suggestions?
- *Briefing*. Is this regular? Does it cover current plans, progress and future developments?
- *Represent*. Am I prepared to represent the feelings of the group when required?
- *Support*. Do I visit people at their work when the team is apart? Do I then represent to the individual the whole team in my manner and encouragement?

Idea 47 – Developing the individual

Go through each heading and question below. If the answers to any are unsatisfactory, draw up a plan to put each of them right. Some you can deal with tomorrow, others you will need to plan.

- *Targets*. Have they been agreed and quantified?
- *Induction*. Does s/he really know the other team members and the organisation?
- *Achievement*. Does s/he know how his/her work contributes to the overall result?

- *Responsibilities*. Has s/he got a clear and accurate job description? Can I delegate more to him/her?
- *Authority*. Does s/he have sufficient authority for his/her task?
- *Training*. Has adequate provision been made for training or retraining both technical and as a team member?
- *Recognition*. Do I emphasise people's successes? In failure is criticism constructive?
- *Growth*. Does s/he see the chance of development? Does s/he see some pattern of career?
- *Performance*. Is this regularly reviewed?
- *Reward*. Are work, capacity and pay in balance?
- *The task*. Is s/he in the right job? Has s/he the necessary resources?
- *The person*. Do I know this person well? What makes him/her different from others?
- *Time/attention*. Do I spend enough with individuals listening, developing, counselling?
- *Grievances*. Are these dealt with promptly?
- *Security*. Does s/he know about pensions, redundancy and so on?
- *Appraisal*. Is the overall performance of each individual regularly reviewed in face-to-face discussion?

The good leader in teambuilding must act as:

- encourager;
- harmoniser;
- compromiser;
- expediter/gatekeeper;
- standard setter;
- group observer/commentator; and
- follower.

Remind yourself

The power of a team to accomplish its mission is directly related to how well the leader selects and develops its members.

Idea 48 – The individual and teams

As leader there must be a clear understanding of:

1 Team properties –
   - common background/history (or lack of it);
   - participation patterns;
   - communication;
   - cohesiveness;
   - atmosphere;
   - standards;
   - structure;
   - organisation;
   - changes over time (forming, storming, norming and performing) both progressive and regressive; and
   - how to change the team properties in evidence.
2 Team roles being defined, but with room left for individual personality.
3 Team member functions –
   - distinction between content (the what) and process (the how) of group functioning;
   - difference between behaviour related to the *task* and behaviour related to *maintenance* of the team and that behaviour which expresses individual *idiosyncrasies*; and
   - team leader functions (as above).

4   The individual –
   • balancing the interests and self-expression of individuals and the team;
   • the value of the task draws individuals/team together; and
   • having sound values motivates individuals in teams.
5   Team processes –
   • to see what is really going on;
   • improved decision-making rests on seeing beneath the surface the pressures that influence the team;
   • calmness creates interdependence within the team and with the leader;
   • avoid team flight into abstractions;
   • aim for consensus (only where possible); and
   • assess team view of authority to see how processes/decisions are being affected by it.
6   Teams within teams –
   • watch out for hostility, communication failure and mistrust as signs of team fragmentation;
   • develop teamwork between teams as well as within them;
   • winning can be as destructive to teams as losing, if not worse, unless both outcomes are handled well; and
   • be aware of teams within teams and act accordingly to regain cohesiveness or sub-divide.

Summary and follow-up test

Setting and achieving your objectives

Summary

In your business/professional and your personal life you must:

- set goals/objectives (short, medium and long-term);
- create plans to achieve them; and
- implement plans to achieve them.

Follow-up test

- Have you defined 'purpose' in your personal and business life?
- Have you identified and set goals and objectives?
- Have you laid plans and started implementing them to achieve goals/objectives?

Decision-making skills

Summary

Do you have a five point plan approach to decision-making and problem-solving?

1 define objectives;
2 check information;
3 develop options;
4 evaluate and decide; and
5 implement.

Follow-up test

In your decision-making and problem-solving, do you use:

1 holistic thinking;
2 thinking in concepts;
3 imagination;
4 analysis;
5 valuing (truth);
6 intuition;
7 your unconscious mind;
8 options; and
9 argument and originality?

Leadership skills

Summary

Leadership centres on:

- the leader – qualities of personality and character;
- the situation – partly constant, partly varying;
- the team – the followers: their needs and values;
- the overlapping needs of the Task, Team and Individual; and
- leadership skills/functions, which can be summarised as:
  - defining the task;
  - planning;
  - briefing;
  - controlling;

- evaluating;
- motivating;
- organising; and
- providing an example.

Follow-up test

- Have you analysed your leadership strengths/weaknesses and addressed your own development needs?
- Have you continuously addressed the functions of leadership?
- Do you constantly focus on Task, Team, Individual?
- Are you getting things done?

Teambuilding

Summary

Teambuilding centres on:

- achieving the task;
- building and maintaining the team; and
- developing the individual.

Follow-up test

- Have you noticed that morale and motivation is up or down in yourself and others?
- Are people working well as individuals and in teams?
- Do individuals have personal development plans?

Part Four

Thinking As A Leader

Introduction

This section of the book looks at ways in which you can ensure that you are creative and innovative as a leader or manager and then examines the key attributes and qualities you need to develop in order to build your personality and character as a leader.

*T*hirteen *G*reatest *I*deas for *C*reativity and *I*nnovation

Idea 49 – Seven obstacles to creativity

There are a number of obstacles which inhibit creativity. The seven main ones are:

1   negativity;
2   fear of failure;
3   lack of quality thinking time;
4   over-conformance with rules and regulations;
5   making assumptions;
6   applying too much logic; and
7   thinking you are not creative.

These obstacles can be seen in this identikit profile of the non-creative person; someone who is:

- not able to think positively about problems (and does not see them as opportunities);
- too busy or stressed to think objectively or at all;
- very self-critical;
- timid in putting forward a new idea (fearing ridicule);
- viewed as a conformist by friends/colleagues;
- prone to apply logic as a first and last resort;
- sceptical that many people are capable of being creative;

- unable to think laterally; and
- uninspired even when confronted with a new idea.

On the other hand, creativity can be encouraged in people (including oneself) by exploring some of the qualities and characteristics of creative thinkers and the activities/ steps that can be undertaken to improve the processes involved.

Ask yourself

How many of the seven obstacles do I recognise in myself? How am I going to overcome them? Which are the easiest ones to deal with first?

Idea 50 – Ten things a creative person ought to be

You *can* learn to be more creative. Here are the suggestions.

1 think beyond the invisible frameworks that surround problems/situations;
2 recognise when assumptions are being made and challenge them;
3 spot blinkered thinking and widen the field of vision (to draw on the experiences of other individuals/businesses);
4 develop/adapt ideas from more than one source;
5 practice serendipity (finding valuable and agreeable things when not particularly seeking them) – having a wide attention span and range of interests is important;
6 'transfer technology' from one field to another;
7 be open/prepared to use chance or unpredictable things/events to advantage;

8   explore thought processes and the key elements of your mind at work in analysing, valuing and synthesising;
9   use your 'depth' mind (the unconscious mind) for example by sleeping on a problem to generate creative solutions to problems; and
10 note down thoughts/ideas that apparently drop into your mind unsolicited so that they are not forgotten.

Remind yourself

Discovery consists of seeing what everyone has seen and thinking what nobody has thought.

Idea 51 – Seven ways to stimulate creativity

1   Use analogy (to improve imaginative thinking) to find 'models' or solutions in 'nature', in existing products/services and/or in other organisations – not always reinventing the wheel.
2   Try, as appropriate, to sometimes make the strange familiar and the familiar strange in order to spark new ideas.
3   Make connections with points that are:
    • apparently irrelevant;
    • disguised/buried or not easily accessible;
    • outside own sphere of expertise; and
    • lacking authority.
4   Suspend judgement to encourage the creative process and avoid premature criticism – analysis and criticism repress creativity.

5 Know when to leave a problem (remaining aware but detached) for solutions to emerge – patience is important here as is the suspension of judgement.
6 Tolerate ambiguity and occasionally live with doubt and uncertainty.
7 Stimulate your own curiosity (in everything including travel) and your skills of observation, listening, reading and recording.

Idea 52 – The four main stages of creativity

1 *Preparation* – information gathering, analysis and solution exploration.
2 *Incubation* – letting the mind work to continue the process.
3 *Illumination* – inspiration; which can come when the individual is not necessarily thinking about the problem but is in a relaxed frame of mind.
4 *Verification* – testing ideas, solutions, hunches, insights for applicability.

Idea 53 – Innovation: the seven key players

It is worth identifying some of the key players who, if they were all present within an organisation, would surely make it unbeatable.

- *Creative thinker* – produces new and original ideas.
- *Innovator* – brings new products/services to the market or changes existing ones.
- *Inventor* – produces new and commercial ideas.
- *Entrepreneur* – conceives or receives ideas and translates them into business reality to exploit a market opportunity.
- *Intrapreneur* – responsible for innovation within an organisation.
- *Champion* – determination and commitment to implement an idea.
- *Sponsor* – backs an idea and helps remove obstacles.

Successful businesses run on change and effective innovation require:

1 a blend of new ideas;
2 the ability to get things done;
3 sound commercial sense;
4 customer focus; and
5 a conducive organisational climate.

Managers should be able to:

- manage for creativity;
- provide an organisational environment in which innovation can thrive; and
- use a variety of techniques to stimulate ideas for products/services/systems and to generate ideas for bringing them to fruition.

The management of innovation (and drawing 'greatness' out of people) must be seen as a process with three phases:

1 the generation of ideas (from individuals and teams);
2 the harvesting of ideas (people evaluating ideas); and
3 the implementation of ideas (teams developing and introducing ideas to the final, customer-satisfied stage).

Management mantra

Creative thinking makes it possible: teamwork makes it happen.

Idea 54 – How to recruit and retain creative people

For the appropriate jobs, of course, you will need creative people and their characteristics tend to be:

- high general intelligence;
- strongly motivated;
- stimulated by challenge;
- vocational in attitude to work;
- able to hold contradictory ideas together in creative tension;
- curious, with good listening and observing skills;
- able to think for themselves, independent in thought;
- neither an introvert nor an extrovert, but rather in the middle; and
- interested in many areas/things.

Creative individuals thrive if they are:

1   appreciated and receive recognition;
2   given freedom to work in their area(s) of greatest interest;
3   allowed contact with stimulating colleagues;
4   given stimulating projects to work on; and
5   free to make mistakes.

Retaining creative people not only requires that their creativity continues to thrive in the right environment, but also that financially they are flexibly and well rewarded and given the freedom to operate and work without being stifled by excess bureaucracy.

Remind yourself

The quality of an innovative organisation depends ultimately on the quality of the people you employ.

Idea 55 – How to encourage creativity

It is not always easy to manage the creative and innovative aspects of teamwork, where individuals ideally need to share the values, characteristics and interests of the other team members, to work with them in harmony and yet have something different to offer.

Belbin identified nine team-member roles, some of which are relatively self-explanatory:

1 plant (solves difficult problems);
2 resource manager;
3 co-ordinator;
4 shaper;
5 monitor/evaluator;
6 team worker (co-operative, diplomatic);
7 implementer;
8 completer; and
9 specialist.

A good team will exhibit all of the above 'roles', not necessarily with nine different people, but with fewer team members adopting different roles to complete the task.

Encouraging creativity in teams (besides helping individuals to 'perform' the Belbin roles within a team) depends on a manager's skills at:

- using the different skills within the team (having first identified the attributes of each individual);
- ensuring conflicts of ideas are allowed to happen and are tolerated by all;
- recognising particularly good contributions;
- helping the team generate ideas (e.g. by brainstorming); and
- creating an open environment where individuals can speak up honestly.

Idea 56 - How communicating can reinforce innovation

Feedback can maintain interest levels and information about progress made can stimulate further activity and more progress. Good communication can help improve creativity and innovation and should:

- stress importance of new ideas and show how business has improved because of their implementation;
- indicate why ideas have been rejected/accepted;
- give progress reports of ideas originated by individuals/teams; and
- recognise and reward appropriately for successful innovation.

Ask yourself

Do people know that I always listen to new ideas?

Idea 57 – Overcoming obstacles to creativity and innovation

Too often good ideas wither on the vine and die. Don't let yours.

If you're not careful, creativity and innovation can be killed off by:

1 an initial response of outright condemnation, ridicule, rejection, damning criticism or faint praise;
2 the vested interest of a particular person or department; or
3 too early an evaluation/judgement – sometimes suspending judgement early on can see an idea grow and reach a strong stage where it will work.

Managers who are creative and act in innovation-friendly ways have not only the usual leadership skills (of defining objectives, planning, controlling, supporting and reviewing in the areas of task, team and individual needs) but also are able to:

- accept risk;
- work with half-formed ideas;
- bend the rules;
- respond quickly; and
- be enthusiastic (to motivate others).

Ask yourself

Do I try to look for the 'good' in an idea rather than only seeing the 'bad'?

Idea 58 – Making your organisation good at innovation

The business organisation itself has to provide an environment in which creativity and innovation can flourish. The five hallmarks of those organisations that actually are good at innovation (and not just paying lip service to it) are:

1   top-level commitment;
2   flexible in organisational structure;
3   tolerant of failure (and not risk averse);
4   encouraging of team work and innovation; and
5   good at open and constructive communication.

Peter Drucker has said that, 'Managing innovation . . . [is a] challenge to management . . . especially top management, and a touchstone of its competence.'

Organisations need to work at the main ingredients for success at managing innovation and apply themselves to the five hallmarks listed above.

1   Top level commitment

This must be visible and audible and top management must ensure that blocks are removed and that inhibiting bureaucracy/individuals does not foul up the process. Chief executives and senior managers must value new ideas and innovation and participate actively to ensure that all know of their commitment to positive and useful change. Sometimes the need for short-term profits can dull the edge of creativity and innovation. Only top management can prevent this happening – taking the long not the short-term view.

2   Flexible in organisational structure

The antithesis of the innovative organisation is the bureaucratic one and Weber's characteristics of bureaucratic organisations are as follows:

- authority is impersonal and formal;
- strong emphasis on functional specialisation;
- a rule for every eventuality;
- strong emphasis on hierarchy and status;
- clearly laid down procedures (red tape);
- proliferation of paperwork; and
- security of employment and advancement by seniority.

At the opposite end of the scale would be the flexible organisation, which is one:

- capable of responding to changing situations;
- where barriers between staff in different areas are minimised;
- with a flat rather than pyramid organisational structure;
- where decision-making is pushed downwards to where the organisation meets its customers/suppliers;
- with entrepreneurial flair present at all levels;
- which can develop and test more than one solution to problems encountered;
- with efficient rather than stifling monitoring systems;
- which has enough 'discipline' to get things done; and
- which balances freedom and order.

3 Tolerant of failure

Innovation and risk go hand in hand. Management that goes into critical overdrive when mistakes occur (rather than analysing them to learn from the failures) smothers creativity and innovation. Risks can yield failure, but not taking risks can spell total disaster and an end to profits and growth.

Unless failure results from negligence, recklessness or complete incompetence, managers should not seek out scapegoats or exact revenge. Profits are the reward for taking risks and innovative organisations learn to live with risk.

4 Encouraging teamwork and innovation

In innovation it can be said that none of us is as good as all of us. Teamwork and innovation are better in organisations where:

- the climate is open;
- participation is encouraged;
- facts and information are readily available;
- change is managed positively;
- resources are provided for training and development;
- rules are at a minimum (with policies and guidelines instead);
- internal communications are good and more by mouth than memo;
- respect is given to all colleagues (but not on demand by management – it has to be earned);
- managers are themselves highly motivated; and
- teamwork often transcends departmental boundaries.

5   Good at open and constructive communication

Communication should be good laterally and vertically (and flatter organisations should – in theory, at least – encourage good lateral communication). Managers should ensure a good flow of information – ideas can emerge as a result. Cross-fertilisation can create more (and better) ideas, particularly where departmental, divisional boundaries are crossed.

Management mantra

None of us is as good as all of us, so build a community of creativity and innovation.

Idea 59 – Checklist for the innovative organisation

- Is the top management team committed to innovation?
- Does the organisation express clearly its vision (which should include an emphasis on innovation)?
- Is the chief executive openly enthusiastic for change?
- Are mutual stimulation, feedback and constructive criticism all at high levels of activity?
- Is the organisation good at teamwork including the use of project teams?
- Are mistakes and failures accepted as part of risk-taking?
- Do creative people join and stay with the organisation?
- Is innovation rewarded (financially or by promotion or both)?
- Are lateral communications good?

- Can ideas be exchanged informally and are opportunities provided to do this?
- Does the organisation raise excuses not to innovate?
- Are resources given to new ideas?
- Is the structure flexible?
- Is decision-making pushed down to the lowest level at which decisions could be taken?
- Do all staff see themselves as part of the creative and innovative processes?
- Does the organisation take a long-term view of the benefits of innovation?
- Is innovation part of the organisation's vision and strategy?
- Is it fun to work in your organisation?

Score your organisation 'yes' or 'no'. If you have got more than nine 'no' scores – it's not good!

Remind yourself

If you take risks, you make mistakes, but if you do not take risks, you are doomed to failure.

Idea 60 - Ways to generate ideas in an organisation

Ask yourself

Do I operate an effective internal market for potentially innovative ideas in my organisation?

It is interesting to note that organisations can get ideas from, amongst other sources:

- R&D (internal or external);
- staff;
- competitors;
- suppliers;
- customers; and
- quality circles.

One survey demonstrated that SMEs (small and medium sized enterprises) can get ideas from, in order of importance:

1 staff;
2 customers;
3 market and competition;
4 board and planning group;
5 sales department;
6 suppliers;
7 managing director;

8 consultants; and
9 shows and exhibitions.

Ideas have to be sieved – by individuals or by teams – to choose and refine the selected ideas to then develop them and take them to market.

Suggestion schemes can work provided people on all sides know that:

- all ideas from everyone will be listened to;
- every idea deserves thanks;
- some ideas will not work; and
- a forum for ideas assists the process of innovation.

Recognition (and selection) of ideas to be pursued should be on the basis that the idea can show:

- originality of thought;
- ultimate benefit to the customer;
- business potential;
- quality improvement;
- cost savings; and
- viability in implementation.

In sieving ideas, three questions should be asked (as Henry Ford did):

1 Is it needed?
2 Is it practical?
3 Is it commercial?

Management mantra

If in doubt, try it out.

Idea 61 – Using brainstorming to generate ideas

Brainstorming (getting a large number of ideas from a group in a short time) can produce ideas (which then have to be sieved and tested) and Alexander Osborn's rules are hard to beat:

- suspend judgement – no criticism or evaluation;
- free-wheel – anything goes, the wilder the better;
- quantity – the more ideas the merrier; and
- combine and improve – link ideas, improve suggested ones.

In leading a brainstorming session the four main steps are:

1 *Introduce* – aim of session and remind people of Osborn's rules.
2 *Warm up* – if necessary do a practice exercise (e.g. 20 uses for a hammer).
3 *State the problem* – not too detailed.
4 *Guide* – time to think:
   - generation of ideas;
   - no judgement/criticism/evaluation!
   - clarify; and
   - maintain free-flow of ideas.

In leading a session that is 'sticky' and short of ideas to start with, ask 'what if?' questions to stimulate thought.

Brainstorming sessions should always be followed up, perhaps in smaller groups and ideas should then be evaluated by:

- deciding the selection criteria;
- selecting obvious winning ideas;
- eliminating the unworkable ideas;
- sifting ideas into groupings and selecting the best in each;
- applying the selection criteria to obvious winners and 'best of' the various groups;
- testing the selections by 'reverse brainstorming' (i.e. in how many ways can this idea fail?); and
- informing the participants of further developments.

Successful brainstorming by managers can be achieved by asking yourself these questions:

1   Do you use it whenever appropriate?
2   Does it work? If not, are you leading it effectively?
3   Is there a better person than you to lead a session?
4   Can you point to where brainstorming sessions have improved creative thinking in your organisation?
5   Do you and your managers have a list of problems that could benefit from brainstorming?
6   Do you use teams sufficiently to work on problems?

In taking good ideas to market here are a number of questions you should apply to your organisation.

Checklist for generation of ideas	YES	NO
Is there an internal market for innovative ideas?	☐	☐
Do teams allocate time to consider ideas?	☐	☐
Do you and your teams spend time away from the office to review performance and plans?	☐	☐
Are customer/suppliers involved in innovation in your business?	☐	☐
Do you have successfully innovative teams and/or individuals and can you identify reasons for their success?	☐	☐
Do you have a suggestion scheme that works?	☐	☐
Are new ideas properly rewarded?	☐	☐
Do you help ensure new ideas are not lost through poor presentation?	☐	☐
Do you know of an alternative route to profitability and growth other than through innovation?	☐	☐

Score your organisation 'yes' or 'no'.

Ask yourself

Do I spend more time on 'brainstorming' than 'blamestorming.'

*T*hree *G*reatest *I*deas for *L*eadership *Q*ualities

Idea 62 – The 25 attributes of leadership and management

A survey of successful chief executives on the attributes most valuable at top levels of management indicated the following *in order of rating*:

1 Ability to take decisions.
2 LEADERSHIP.
3 Integrity.
4 Enthusiasm.
5 Imagination.
6 Willingness to work hard.
7 Analytical ability.
8 Understanding of others.
9 Ability to spot opportunities.
10 Ability to meet unpleasant situations.
11 Ability to adapt quickly to change.
12 Willingness to take risks.
13 Enterprise.
14 Capacity to speak lucidly.
15 Astuteness.
16 Ability to administer efficiently.

17   Open-mindedness.
18   Ability to 'stick to it'.
19   Willingness to work long hours.
20   Ambition.
21   Single-mindedness.
22   Capacity for lucid writing.
23   Curiosity.
24   Skill with numbers.
25   Capacity for abstract thought.

Ask yourself

Am I good at giving direction, providing inspiration, building teams, setting an example and being accepted?

Idea 63 – The seven qualities of leadership

A leader is the kind of person (with leadership qualities) who has the appropriate knowledge and skill to lead a group to achieve its ends *willingly*.

Personality and character cannot be left out of leadership. There are certain generic leadership traits and seven important ones are:

1   Enthusiasm: try naming a leader without it!
2   Integrity: meaning both personal wholeness and sticking to values outside yourself, primarily goodness and truth – integrity makes people trust a leader.

3 Toughness: demanding, with high standards, resilient, tenacious and with the aim of being respected (not necessarily popular).
4 Fairness: impartial, rewarding/penalising performance without 'favourites', treating individuals differently but equally.
5 Warmth: the heart as well as the mind being engaged, loving what is being done and caring for people – cold fish do not make good leaders.
6 Humility: the opposite of arrogance, being a listener and without an overwhelming ego.
7 Confidence: not over-confident (which leads to arrogance), but with self-confidence – people know whether you have or have not got it.

Idea 64 – Leadership qualities test

In testing whether or not you have the basic qualities of leadership, you should ask yourself these questions:

- Do I possess the seven qualities outlined in *Idea 63* above? (This 'test' will sub-sequently reveal whether or not you really do!)
- Have I demonstrated that I am a responsible person?
- Do I like the responsibility and the rewards of leadership?
- Am I well known for my enthusiasm at work?
- Have I ever been described as having integrity?
- Can I show that people think of me as a warm person?
- Am I an active and socially participative person?
- Do I have the self-confidence to take criticism, indifference and/or unpopularity from others?
- Can I control my emotions and moods or do I let them control me?
- Have I been dishonest or less than straight with people who work for me over the past six months?

- Am I very introvert, or very extrovert (or am I an ambivert – a mixture of both – as leaders should be)?

If leadership depends on the situation, you need to ask yourself, whatever your qualities, whether you are right for the situation:

- Are your interests, aptitudes and temperament suited to your current field of work?
- If not, can you identify one that would better suit you where you would emerge as a leader?
- Do you have the 'authority of knowledge' in your current field (and have you acquired all the necessary professional and specialist skills through training that you could have done at this point in your career)?
- Are you experienced in more than one field/industry/function?
- Are you interested in fields adjacent and relevant to your own?
- Do you read situations well and are you flexible in your approach to changes within your field?

Summary and follow-up test

Creativity and innovation

Summary

The seven habits of successful creative thinkers are:

1 thinking outside the apparent confines of the problem/situation;
2 welcoming chance intrusions;
3 listening to your unconscious mind;

4   suspending judgement;
5   using the stepping stones of analogy;
6   tolerating ambiguity; and
7   banking all ideas from all sources

Innovation needs the generation, harvesting and implementation of ideas. Managers good at innovation accept risk, are flexible and are motivated to take ideas through to completion.

Follow-up test

- Do you now deal in ideas generated from many different sources?
- Have you created a creative and innovative environment for the free generation of ideas?
- Is creativity and innovation encouraged in individuals, teams and task completion?
- Is your organisation committed to innovation from the top, tolerant of failure and encouraging of creativity and innovation at all levels?
- Is internal communication about innovation good?
- What creative/innovative initiatives can you enumerate as having happened?

Leadership qualities

Summary

Seven important qualities of leadership are:

1   enthusiasm;
2   integrity;
3   toughness;

4   fairness;

5   warmth;

6   humility; and

7   confidence.

Follow-up test

You should regularly answer the questions posed in *Idea 64*.

Part Five

Power Through The People

Introduction

Worthwhile results can only be achieved with other people and this section looks at how to get the best from other people, particularly examining how best to motivate people including yourself!

*S*ixteen *G*reatest *I*deas for *G*etting the *B*est from your *T*eam

Idea 65 – Adair's eight rules for motivating people

1 Be motivated yourself.
2 Select people who are highly motivated.
3 Treat each person as an individual.
4 Set realistic and challenging targets.
5 Remember that progress motivates.
6 Create a motivating environment.
7 Provide fair rewards.
8 Give recognition.

Ask yourself

Have I moved on yet from the 'carrot and stick' reward and fear approach to motivation?

Idea 66 – 50:50 rule of motivation

Just as the Pareto principle (or 80:20 rule) is the ratio of 'the vital few and trivial many', the Adair 50:50 rule has it that:

- 50% of motivation comes from within a person; and
- 50% from his or her environment, especially from the leadership encountered in it.

Unfortunately human behaviour and what decides/triggers it is more complicated than the carrot and stick 'theory', which deals only with external stimuli. The 'carrot' of reward/incentive and the 'stick' of fear of consequences reveal only two 'motives' that govern action. There are many more!

The expectancy theory – formulated by Edward C Tolman in the 1930s – whereby behaviour rests on the instinctive tendency for individuals to balance the value of expected benefits against the expenditure of energy – falls into the same 'stimulus-response' approach to motivation. It does demonstrate, however, that an individual's strength of motivation can be affected by the expectations of outcomes from certain actions and further strengthened by the individual's preferred outcome, as demonstrated by Victor H. Vroom in the 1960s.

It pays, therefore, in external stimuli to bear in mind that:

1   the routes to desired outcomes for individuals and teams are clear; and
2   individuals perceive the rewards or punishments in different ways according to their own values.

This confirms the need to treat people as individuals but as the 50:50 rule also indicates, other motivational factors should always be set in the context of the individual's *managed environment*. Other theories of motivation which suggest that 90% of motivation is within an individual should be tempered by the 50:50 rule.

Management mantra

You get more of the behaviour you reward.

Idea 67 – Maslow's hierarchy of needs

A sketch map of individual needs – which is useful for managers when considering individuals – can be drawn from Maslow's hierarchy of needs (1954), but it must be borne in mind that his theory does not fully appreciate individual differences or that each person has a unique set of needs and values.

Maslow identified five motivating factors in his hierarchy of needs and indicated that as each need is satisfied, others then emerge. He identified:

1 physiological needs (including hunger, thirst, sleep);
2 safety needs (security and protection from danger);
3 social needs (belonging, acceptance, social life, friendship and love);
4 self-esteem (self-respect, achievement, status, recognition); and
5 self-actualisation (growth, accomplishment, personal development).

However, points to bear in mind are that:

- individuals do not necessarily move up the hierarchy on the principle that a 'satisfied need ceases to motivate' although that can be the case;
- different levels of needs can kick in at random points on the scale toward full satisfaction of needs;
- culture and age and other factors can affect the importance of the different needs to different people and at different stages in their lives; and

- the satisfying of some needs can be sacrificed in order to try and satisfy higher level needs.

Remind yourself

Use Maslow's needs as a sketch map – no more – of individual needs; and as a leader, consider them in relation to each member of your team.

Idea 68 – McGregor's theory X and theory Y

In 1960 in his book, *The Human Side of Enterprise,* McGregor demonstrated that the way in which managers manage depends on the assumptions made about human behaviour. He grouped these assumptions into Theory X and Theory Y.

Theory X – the traditional view of direction and control

1 The average human being has an inherent dislike of work and will avoid it if possible.
2 Because of this dislike of work, most people must be coerced, controlled, directed, threatened with punishment to get them to give adequate effort toward the achievement of organisational objectives.
3 The average human being prefers to be directed, wishes to avoid responsibility, has relatively little ambition and wants security above all.

Theory Y – the integration of individual and organisational goals

1 The expenditure of physical and mental effort in work is as natural as play or rest.
2 External control and the threat of punishment are not the only means for bringing about effort toward organisational objectives. People will exercise self-direction and self-control in the service of objectives to which they are committed.
3 Commitment to objectives is a function of the rewards associated with their achievement.
4 The average human being learns, under proper conditions, not only to accept, but to seek responsibility.
5 The capacity to exercise a relatively high degree of imagination, ingenuity and creativity in the solution of organisational problems is widely, not narrowly, distributed in the population.
6 Under the conditions of modern industrial life, the intellectual potentialities of the average human being are only partially utilised.

McGregor drew on Maslow for much of Theory Y and put forward the cluster of features as an unproven hypothesis and further research was needed (Herzberg) to seek to prove it correct.

In terms of management in practice Theory Y does reveal that in any individual within an organisation *there are untapped resources of goodwill, energy, creativity and intelligence.*

Idea 69 – Herzberg's motivation-hygiene theory

In Herzberg's research (published in his 1959 book *The Motivation to Work*), fourteen factors were identified to be the sources of good or bad feelings:

1   recognition;
2   achievement;
3   possibility of growth;
4   advancement;
5   salary;
6   interpersonal relations;
7   supervision – technical;
8   responsibility;
9   company policy and administration;
10 working conditions;
11 work itself;
12 factors in personal life;
13 status; and
14 job security.

The eight *hygiene factors*, according to Herzberg, which can create job *dissatisfaction* are:

1   Company policy and administration:
    • availability of clearly defined policies, especially those relating to people; and
    • adequacy of organisation and management.
2   Supervision:
    • technical; and
    • accessibility, competence and fairness of your superior.
3   Interpersonal relations:
    • relations with supervisors, subordinates and colleagues; and
    • quality of social life at work.
4   Salary:
    • total compensation package, such as wages, salary, pension, company car and other financially related benefits.

5 Status:
- a person's position or rank in relation to others, symbolised by title, size of office or other tangible elements.

6 Job security:
- freedom from insecurity, such as loss of position or loss of employment altogether.

7 Personal life:
- the effect of a person's work on family life, e.g. stress, unsocial hours or moving house.

8 Working conditions:
- the physical conditions in which you work;
- the amount of work;
- facilities available; and
- environmental aspects e.g. ventilation, light, space, tools, noise.

The six *motivating factors* that lead to job *satisfaction* were identified by Herzberg as being:

1 Achievement:
- specific successes, such as the successful completion of a job, solutions to problems, vindication and seeing the results of your work.

2 Recognition:
- any act of recognition, whether notice or praise (separating recognition and reward from recognition with no reward).

3 Possibility of growth:
- changes in job where professional growth potential is increased.

4 Advancement:
- changes which enhance position or status at work.

5 Responsibility:
- being given real responsibility, matched with necessary authority to discharge it.

6   The work itself:
  • the actual doing of the job or phases of it.

The hygiene factors are those where people seek to avoid particular situations, whereas the motivating factors are matched with peoples needs to achieve self-actualisation or self-realisation.

Satisfaction of the Herzberg motivators and avoidance of problems with the hygiene factors can help you as a manager to assess roles and jobs within your organisation to check what job enrichment or empowerment you ought to contemplate to improve performance and give individuals greater job satisfaction.

Ask yourself

How do Maslow, McGregor and Herzberg work for my team members AND how do they work for ME?

Idea 70 – Manager's motivating checklist

There are five key elements that you should constantly review if you want to ensure that individuals stay motivated:

1   a sense of achievement in their job and the feeling that they are making a worthwhile contribution to the objective of the team;
2   jobs that are challenging and demanding with responsibilities to match capabilities;
3   adequate recognition for achievements;

4   control over delegated duties; and
5   a feeling that they are developing along with growing experience and ability.

Remind yourself

Achievement, recognition, work itself, responsibility and advancement – all add up to the growth (self-actualisation) dimension of a job.

Idea 71 – Ten ways to strengthen your own motivation

To motivate others successfully you've got to feel highly motivated yourself – there are ways to do just that:

1   to feel and act enthusiastically and in a committed way in your work;
2   to take responsibility when things go wrong rather than blaming others;
3   to identify ways you can lead by example;
4   to act on the 50:50 principle;
5   to motivate by word and example rather than manipulation;
6   set an example naturally rather than in a calculated way;
7   not to give up easily;
8   to ensure you are in the right job for your own abilities, interests and temperament;
9   to be able to cite experiences where what you have said or done has had an inspirational effect on individuals, the team or the organisation; and
10 to remember always that the three badges of leadership are enthusiasm, commitment and perseverance.

Idea 72 – The seven indicators of high motivation

1 *Energy* – not necessarily extrovert but alertness and quiet resolve.
2 *Commitment* – to the common purpose.
3 *Staying power* – in the face of problems/difficulties/setbacks.
4 *Skill* – possession of skills indicates aims and ambitions.
5 *Single-mindedness* – energy applied in a single direction.
6 *Enjoyment* – goes hand in hand with motivation.
7 *Responsibility* – willingness to seek and accept it.

Idea 73 – Choosing people with motivation – the Michelangelo motive

Choosing people well (and when mistakes are made they should be confronted and remedied early) means looking at motivation, ability and personality and you should, when interviewing, look for real evidence behind the interviewee's facade.

Looking for the 'Michelangelo motive' (where the quality of the work itself is a key motivator) can yield good results in selecting highly motivated individuals. You should look for:

- a sense of pride in the individual's own work;

- an attention to detail;
- a willingness to 'walk the extra mile' to get things right;
- a total lack of the 'its good enough, let it go' mentality;
- an inner direction or responsibility for the work (without the need for supervision); and
- an ability to assess and evaluate own work, independently from the opinions of others.

It should be stressed that perfectionism is not what is called for – the best can be the enemy of the good.

Managers should check whether individuals are in the right job with the right skills and abilities, otherwise motivation techniques will fail. The aim is to select people who are motivated for the most appropriate job.

Management mantra

Select people who are already motivated.

Idea 74 – The key to motivating: treat each person as an individual

Find out what motivates an individual, do not rely on generalised theories or assumptions. Enter into a dialogue with each team member – help them to clarify what it is that motivates them – and use what you find to mutual benefit.

In each person you should engender a sense of:

- trust;
- autonomy;
- initiative;
- industry;
- integrity; and
- security.

Take time with each individual to:

- encourage;
- hearten;
- inspire;
- support;
- embolden; and
- stimulate.

Management mantra

To motivate others, you must be motivated yourself.

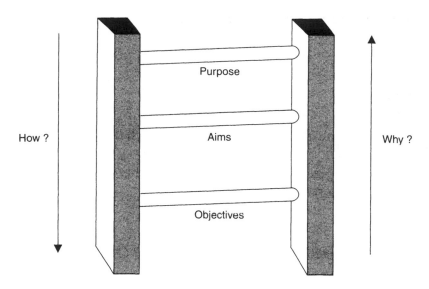

Idea 75 – Using Jacob's ladder to set realistic and challenging targets

Setting realistic targets can only be done in the context of understanding the organisation's aims or purpose. It is only then that targets and objectives can be identified and tasks defined.

Moving down the ladder, ask, 'how are we going to achieve the task?' The answer is by breaking down the purpose into the main aims and the main aims into short and long-term objectives or goals.

Moving up the ladder, ask, 'why are we doing this?' The answer is to achieve this objective in order to achieve this aim and to satisfy this purpose.

Targets set (for short and longer-term objectives) should be:

- specific;
- clear; and
- time-bounded.

An objective or target must be realistic (feasible) and challenging. If you aim for the best you can often get it.

Targets must be agreed and monitored with further action agreed to maintain motivation toward shared objectives.

Idea 76 – Give feedback to reinforce and motivate

Feedback on progress (or even the relative lack of it) helps motivation, either to spur people on, or to concentrate the mind on what yet needs to be done.

Feedback is not given at all or sometimes not often enough, usually for these reasons:

- 'People don't need to be told how they are doing, they already know.'
- 'People take it easy if you say things are going well.'
- 'They are unhappy and cause trouble if you say things are not going well.'
- 'We lack the skills or the time to do it.'

Feedback that is affirmative – praise – must be:

- accurate;
- sincere;
- generous;

- spontaneous; and
- fair.

It must not be:

- patronising;
- superior/condescending;
- grudging; or
- calculated for effect.

Maintaining motivation depends on informing and inspiring and the rule is always to give information first, before you attempt to encourage.

Remind yourself

Giving feedback strengthens motivation.

Idea 77 – Maintain morale to maintain motivation

Maintaining high morale is key to high motivation and morale covers the individuals and the team. Where an individual has low morale, the issues have to be addressed on an individual basis, but where group or team morale is low, the answer lies in deciding whether there is a lack of confidence:

- of ultimate success;
- in the present plan(s);

- in the leadership/management; and
- in the minds of team members.

Remind yourself

Morale covers both attitude and purpose/energy.

It can be necessary to remotivate the team by rebuilding self-confidence and by readdressing:

- aims – and clarifying objectives;
- plans and resources needed;
- leadership;
- overlooked factors;
- re-establishment of the worth or value of the task(s); and
- involvement of individuals in key decisions.

Ask yourself

Is individual and/or team morale high or low? What action should I or other team members take?

Idea 78 – Create a motivating environment

Make sure you create as motivating an environment as you can by observing these nine key points.

1 Beware of creating a restrictive organisation with an over-emphasis on controls.
2 Avoid public criticisms of individuals.
3 Ensure Herzberg's hygiene factors are catered for – the physical and psychological well being of people should have high priority.
4 Control systems should only be introduced where necessary.
5 Give people an input into decisions that affect their working lives (especially in respect of substantial change).
6 Keep units and sub-units as small as possible (large units tend to be bureaucratic and demotivational if they lack inspired leaders).
7 Pay attention to job design – avoid repetitive work, introduce variety.
8 Give people autonomy and a job with a 'product' that an individual can recognise as his/her own.
9 Ensure an individual understands the significance of their job in relation to the whole, which will also encourage new ideas and innovation.

Idea 79 – Give fair rewards to the motivated

Although it is difficult to ensure that the financial reward an individual receives is fair (commensurate with contribution), effort must be applied in trying to get it right. There are other motivating 'returns' that individuals look for from jobs (as in Maslow's hierarchy of needs), but money is the one that has the main strategic importance for most people.

Most individuals like the combination of a fixed salary with a variable element related to performance or profits.

Also of tactical importance are incentives to improve performance in key areas e.g. sales, customer service and credit control.

Incentives can be in the form of cash, vouchers, merchandise or travel, but care must be taken to administer any incentive schemes fairly and without risking demotivating any 'losers'.

In providing fair rewards, an organisation should ask itself:

1. Do we have a scheme whereby financial reward is made up of a fixed and variable element?
2. Do we link performance and pay?
3. Have we addressed the problems of whether to pay performance-related elements to the team or the individual?
4. Do we actively consider changing our information systems to improve methods of rewarding performance?
5. Do we have schemes other than for sales people?
6. Does our organisation reward the behaviours/performance that publicly it values?
7. Do senior managers have pay rises/bonuses when they expect others to do without them?

Remind yourself

It is always worth remembering Herzberg's insight that salary has more power to make people dissatisfied or unhappy than it has the power to motivate them.

Idea 80 – Give recognition to the motivated

Financial reward is seen by the recipient as a tangible form of recognition. There are other ways whereby appreciation is expressed for what has been contributed.

If recognition is not given, an individual can feel unnoticed, unvalued and unrewarded. This leads to a drop in motivation and energy levels. Recognition should be formal or informal, for the individual and/or the team, as appropriate.

In giving recognition, you should try to ensure that you:

1   treat everyone in a fair and equal way;
2   reward real achievements or contributions;
3   reflect the core values of the organisation;
4   use it to guide and encourage all concerned;
5   give it in public if possible;
6   give it formally and informally; and
7   give it genuinely and sincerely.

Other than financial payments, any words of recognition could be reinforced by giving:

- time off (with pay);
- tickets for an event or dinner out;
- a small gift;
- a special project of importance; and
- a change in job title.

It is a good idea to back up words of praise or recognition with some tangible gift.

Find out what is going on, share praise received with subordinates, and say thank-you more often, because people really value positive recognition and are motivated by it.

Remind yourself

To say thank you for good work and give positive feedback

Summary and follow-up test

Summary

To draw the best out of people you need to:

- be motivated yourself;
- select people who are already motivated;
- set challenging but realistic targets;
- remember that progress motivates;
- treat each person as an individual;
- provide fair rewards; and
- give recognition.

Follow-up test

- Do you consciously try to motivate people by understanding their needs and aspirations?
- Are you motivated?
- Do you feel you are getting the best from people?
- Are targets set and monitored with feedback being clearly given?
- Do you spend time with individuals and teams working on motivating them?

Management mantra

Be sparing with praise but liberal with thanks.

Part Six

Getting The Message Across

Introduction

Great leaders and great managers are all effective communicators both one-on-one and in larger groups, using the written or spoken word as appropriate. Unless you can get your message across and take on board what others are trying to tell you, then you simply will not be effective as a leader or manager.

To be a good communicator, you need to develop your personal communication skills, your ability to lead communication groups and your effectiveness in the downward, upward and sideways flows of information and ideas in organisations.

You need to develop your understanding of the nature of communication and the four skills of speaking, listening, writing and reading, particularly as they can be used in interviews, meetings and communicating organisations.

Twenty Greatest Ideas for Effective Communication

Idea 81 – Adair's 15 key issues in communication

It is self evident that written and spoken communication skills are of crucial importance in business (and personal) life. Managers and leaders must be effective communicators, good at getting their message across and at drawing the best out of people. Communication skills in all forms, including non-verbal, need to be worked at and improved to ensure you understand people and they understand you.

1   You must be in social contact with the other person or people.
2   You must want to communicate.
3   It is better to risk familiarity than be condemned to remoteness.
4   The best way to empower others is to impart information (along with the delegated authority to make decisions and act on the information given).
5   Get out of your office – meet, listen, provide information and give people the context in which they operate – to communicate and encourage.
6   Good communication is the core of customer care.
7   Remember customers (and suppliers) communicate with others about you.
8   To communicate with your customers you must handle complaints (as an organisation) as personally as possible – by a meeting or phone call in preference to letter or fax; you must listen to what customers suggest and communicate product/ service changes/developments with them in advance.

9 Presentation skills are important in communicating with colleagues as well as customers/clients.

10 Meetings, internal and external are key indicators of a person's communication (including listening) skills.

11 Communication is a business requirement: establish proper systems and ensure all use them.

12 Remember the equation: size + geographical distance = communication problems.

13 Communicate with poor performers to improve their contribution and in appraisals be truthful, helpful and tactful.

14 Help others to improve their communication skills.

15 Assess your own communication skills and strive to improve them bit by bit. (Also, assess the communication skills of colleagues and identify areas for improvement.)

Management mantra

Don't assume that communication is actually happening.

Idea 82 – Personal communication skills checklist

- Do you understand the importance of communication in your personal and business life?
- Are you a good communicator? (Check with your partner at home, with friends and with colleagues.)
- Can you write down your strengths and weaknesses as a communicator? And have you listed them?

- Have you identified a need to improve your communication skills in any or all of these areas within your organisation, and will you now set about doing so? (reading further books and/or attending training seminars as needs be):
  - listening;
  - reading;
  - writing;
  - one-to-one communication;
  - speaking and presentation; and
  - managing meetings.

Are you motivated strongly to become an excellent communicator?

Idea 83 – Listening – a key element in communication

Listening has been called the forgotten skill in communication. It is more than just hearing, it is the giving of thoughtful attention to another person whilst they are speaking.

The 'disease of not listening' – the 'I hear what you say' response – exhibits the following symptoms:

- Selective listening which is habit forming, not wanting to know things and turning a deaf ear to certain types of information does two things:
  - you do not listen to important items; and
  - people censor what they tell you and both can be damaging in business and in private life.
- The constant interrupter is not listening (but planning his/her own next interruption).
- The 'day-dreamer' is not a listener.

- The poor listener is easily distracted by external factors e.g. noise, heat/cold.
- The lazy listener makes no effort with difficult information.
- The poor listener overreacts to a speaker's delivery and/or quality of visual aids rather than concentrating on what is being said.

The tell-tale signs of a good listener:

- paying close attention to others when they are talking;
- taking an interest in someone you meet for the first time, trying to find an area of mutual interest;
- believing everyone has something of value to teach or impart to you;
- setting aside a person's personality/voice in order to concentrate on what they know;
- being curious in people, ideas and things;
- encouraging a speaker (with nods or eye contact);
- taking notes;
- knowing one's own prejudices and working at controlling them to ensure listening continues;
- being patient with poor communicators;
- not being told you don't listen; and
- having an open mind in respect of other peoples' points of view.

Remind yourself

People have two eyes and two ears and only one tongue – which suggests that they ought to look and also listen twice as much as they speak.

Idea 84 – Being a better listener – developing listening skills

Listening skills centre on the five following attributes:

1 being willing to listen;
2 clearly hearing the message;
3 interpreting the meaning (the speaker's meaning, not only your interpretation);
4 evaluating carefully (suspending judgement at first but then assessing value and usefulness); and
5 responding appropriately – remembering communication is a two-way street.

In active listening you must be prepared to:

- ask questions;
- weigh the evidence;
- watch your assumptions; and
- listen between the lines (at what is not said and for non-verbal elements such as facial expressions, tone, posture, physical gestures etc.).

Idea 85 – Reading skills – must, should and might

Good reading is listening in action – giving time and thought and remaining alert to the possibilities suggested. A good reader will try to work past:

- poor structure and layout;
- boring style;
- off-putting tone;

- too much or too little information;
- content that is difficult to follow;
- inordinate length; and
- lack of illustrations/diagrams.

You should examine what materials you *must* read, *should* read or *might* read in the light of your job/role/future ambitions and then decide accordingly how and when to handle a particular item.

Speed reading is useful but only if it is accompanied by speed understanding, and reading too fast (or too slowly) can impair understanding.

Read selectively (according to the 'must', 'should' or 'might' categorisation) from each item that confronts you. In this, scanning can help decide what attention to give particular items, so you should look at overall content (headings and sub-headings), sample the style and content of a few paragraphs, scan (if still interested) selected parts and then read that which you decide you are interested in. In reading carefully, you should be aware of the need to:

- be clear about your purpose of reading any piece of writing;
- have questions in mind;
- keep the questions firmly in mind and seek answers to them;
- read for main ideas;
- test the evidence, explanations and conclusions critically;
- make notes as you progress;
- test the writer's experience against your own;
- consider whether or not to re-read;
- discuss the material with others if appropriate; and
- reflect on what has been read.

> **Management mantra**
>
> Reading is to the mind what exercise is to the body.

Idea 86 – Writing skills – talking to a person on paper

Communicating in writing is an essential part of your job. There are three key elements in communicating on paper:

- structure and layout;
- content; and
- style and tone.

Writing should be thought of as talking to a person on paper and the six principles of good spoken communication apply – and they are:

1 clarity;
2 planning and preparation;
3 simplicity;
4 vividness;
5 naturalness; and
6 conciseness.

In letters, reports and memos the quality improves if the appropriate amount of planning is given to the points you wish to make and their order of importance. Further drafts can improve on the initial effort.

In writing a business letter you should always test the draft to ensure that:

1 the message is clear;
2 points are made in the best order;
3 it has the right style and tone;
4 the most appropriate words and phrases are being used;
5 the grammar/spelling is correct; and
6 the layout is attractive.

In writing reports that work, the following points should be borne in mind:

- If the report is to stand alone and not to support a briefing or presentation it will need to be more than an aide-memoire.
- A report should:
  - have an introduction with background and objectives;
  - have a title which indicates its purpose;
  - be structured like a book with chapters, headings and sub-headings all clearly numbered and signposted;
  - ensure the main body of evidence is succinct and arranged in an easy-to-follow order;
  - end with conclusions and recommendations;
  - indicate assumptions made;
  - put complicated data into an appendix; and
  - use illustrations/diagrams to clarify points made.

Management mantra

Have something to say and say it or write it as clearly as you can.

Idea 87 – Churchill's guidelines for report writing

Churchill's guidelines for report writing centred on:

- setting out main points in a series of short, crisp paragraphs;
- putting complicated factors or statistics into an appendix;
- considering submitting headings only, to be expanded orally;
- avoiding woolly phrases, opting for conversational phrases; and
- setting out points concisely to aid clearer thinking.

Idea 88 – Test written reports for effectiveness

Reports can be tested for their effectiveness as follows:

- Is the structure and layout clear and easy to follow?
- Is the content complete and does it:
  - state the purpose?
  - say when, by whom, for whom and with what scope it was prepared?
  - identify and address the problem clearly?
  - ensure detail does not cloud the main issue?
  - give sources for facts?
  - use consistent symbols and abbreviations?
  - use accurate figures?
  - make clear statements?
  - have conclusions which flow logically from facts and their interpretation?
  - ensure other possible solutions are only abandoned with stated reasons?
- In general:
  - is the report objective?

- are criticisms of its recommendations pre-empted?
- is it efficient and business-like?
- does it offend anyone?
- can it be understood by a non-technical person?
- is it positive and constructive?
- does it point up the decision to be made and by whom?

The style and tone of written communications is important to ensure the message is put over, and received, clearly. Some rules are:

- keep it simple;
- strive for clarity above all things (even above brevity);
- be natural;
- be concise;
- let the tone reflect your true feelings but beware being terse, curt, sarcastic, peevish, angry, suspicious, insulting, accusing, patronising or presumptuous; and
- be courteous (cordial and tactful).

Ask yourself

What would I make of this report if I received it?

Idea 89 – Adair's six principles of effective speaking

1 Be clear.
2 Be prepared.

3   Be simple.
4   Be vivid.
5   Be natural.
6   Be concise.

Preparation is helped by asking the who/what/how/when/where/why? of the speaking occasion to focus on the audience, the place, the time, the reasons giving rise to the occasion, the information that needs to be covered and how best to put it across.

Idea 90 – Profile the occasion – the first element of a good presentation

When planning a presentation, there is one thing you should do before anything else: profile the occasion, audience and location.

You should ask yourself the following questions.

The occasion

- What kind is it?
- What are the aims of it?
- What time is allowed?
- What else is happening?

The audience

- Do they know anything about you?
- Do you know its size?
- What do they expect?
- Why are they there?
- What is their knowledge level?
- Do you know any personally/professionally?
- Do you expect friendliness, indifference or hostility?
- Will they be able to use what they hear?

The location

- Do you know the room size, seating arrangements, lay-out/set-up and acoustics?
- Do you know the technical arrangements for use of microphones, audio-visuals, lighting, and whether assistance is available (and have you notified in advance your requirements)?
- Do you know who will control room temperature, lighting and moving people in and out?
- Have you seen it/should you see it?

Ask yourself

When making a presentation, do I always check the occasion, the audience and the location?

Idea 91 – Plan and write the presentation

The key elements in planning and writing your presentation are these:

- Deciding your objective, which needs to be:
  - clear;
  - specific;
  - measurable;
  - achievable in the time available;
  - realistic;
  - challenging;
  - worthwhile; and
  - participative.
- Making a plan with a framework which has:
  - a beginning (including introductory remarks, statement of objectives and relevance and an outline of the presentation(s));
  - a middle (divided into up to six sections maximum, ensuring main points are illustrated and supported by examples or evidence, use summaries and consider time allocation carefully – and test it); and
  - an end (summarise, linking conclusions with objectives and end on a high note).

Remind yourself

Light a flame at the start of your presentation and keep it burning throughout.

Idea 92 – Use visual aids in presentations

As up to 50 per cent of information is taken in through the eyes, careful consideration should be given to the clear, simple and vivid use of audio-visuals.

Useful tips are:

- overhead/projector slides help make a point and keep eye contact with an audience (look at the people not the slides);
- only present essential information in this way (keep content to about 25 words or equivalent if in figures);
- have them prepared with appropriate professionalism;
- know the order;
- use pictures and colour if possible; and
- do not leave a visual aid on for too long.

Some difficulties with the different types of audio-visual equipment are:

- *Overhead projection.* Ease of use and flexibility can be offset by poor quality images and problems in using well.
- *35mm slide projection.* Professional in appearance, good for large audience and easy to use with a remote control can be offset by the need for dim lights (making note-taking difficult) and lack of flexibility in changing order of viewing.
- *Flipcharts.* Are easy to use and informal but difficult to use successfully with large groups and generally do not look professional and take up time to use.
- *Computers, tape decks or videos.* Can provide variety but difficult to set up and synchronise, especially without technical support.

Management mantra

A picture is worth a thousand words.

Idea 93 – Prepare your talk – don't prepare to fail

In preparing your talk you need to decide whether you are to present with a full script, notes or from memory. This depends on the occasion and purpose of the presentation but whichever method is chosen, it is always acceptable to refer to your fuller notes if needs be during a presentation. Notes on cards or on slides/flipcharts can be used as memory joggers if you present without notes. If you are required to read a paper, at least be able to look up occasionally. Remember that failing to prepare is preparing to fail.

Idea 94 – Rehearse a presentation

Rehearsal is important, but not so much that spontaneity is killed and naturalness suffers, to ensure the presentation (and any audio-visual aid) is actually going to work in practice.

You should always visit the location if at all possible and check that everything works – knowing the location is as important as rehearsing the presentation, indeed it is an essential part of the rehearsal.

Idea 95 – How best to deliver your presentation on the day

Overall you should ensure that your presentation's:

- *beginning* introduces yourself properly, captures the audience and gives the background, objectives and outline of your talk;
- *middle* is kept moving along (indicating whether questions are to be asked as-you-go or at the end) with eye contact over the whole audience, at a reasonable pace, with a varying voice and obvious enjoyment on your part;
- *end* is signalled clearly and then goes off with a memorised flourish;
- *questions* are audible to all (or repeated if not), answered with conciseness, stimulated by yourself asking some questions, dealt with courteously and with the lights on; and
- *conclusion* is a strong summary of talk and questions/discussions and closes with words of thanks.

If you find you are nervous – and this is normal – experiencing fear and its physical manifestations, remember to:

1 breathe deeply;
2 manage your hands;
3 look at your audience;
4 move well;
5 talk slowly;
6 compose and relax yourself;
7 remember that the audience is invariably on your side; and
8 project forward to the end of the presentation and picture the audience applauding at the end.

> **Remind yourself**
>
> Be clear, be simple, be vivid and be natural.

Idea 96 – One-to-one interviews

One-to-one meetings have common characteristics in that they are (usually) pre-arranged, require preparation and have a definite purpose.

Unless it happens to be a dismissal, one-to-one interviews require that:

- both parties know the purpose of the meeting (notified in advance);
- information to be exchanged should be considered in advance and answers at the meeting should be honest; and
- as interviewer you should keep control: stick to the point at the issue and the time allocated and give the other party adequate time to talk (prompting by questions if necessary).

The structure of the interview should be as follows:

- the opening – setting the scene, the purpose and a relaxed atmosphere;
- the middle – stay with the purpose, listen, cover the agenda; and
- the close – summary, agree action, end naturally not abruptly on a positive note.

Sometimes it is useful to ask the right questions to obtain the required information/ exchange. Questions to use are the open-ended, prompting, probing, or what-if questions, whilst the ones to avoid (unless being used for specific reasons) are the yes/ no, closed, leading or loaded questions.

Ask yourself

Do I know the purpose of this interview? Does the other person?

Idea 97 – Seven ways to give criticism

In performance-appraisal interviews the aim should be to give constructive criticism in the following way:

1 in private;
2 without preamble;
3 simply and accurately;
4 only of actions that can be changed;
5 without comparison with others;
6 with no reference to other people's motives; and
7 without apology if given in good faith.

Idea 98 – Seven ways to receive criticism

In receiving constructive criticism you should:

1 remain quiet and listen;
2 not find fault with the criticising person;
3 not manipulate the appraiser by your response (e.g. despair);
4 not try to change the subject;

5   not caricature the complaint;
6   not ascribe an ulterior motive to the appraiser; and
7   give the impression you understand the point.

In handling criticism you should accept it and not ignore, deny or deflect it.

Ask yourself

Can I take criticism myself?

Idea 99 – Communication and the management of meetings

Meetings are much maligned, but are they usually approached and handled as they should be? In general terms, if it is to work, any meeting needs:

- planning;
- informality;
- participation;
- purpose; and
- leadership.

That is the case, whether the meeting is in committee or conference format.

A meeting must have a purpose and this can be one (or all) of the following:

- to pool available information;
- to make decisions;
- to let off steam/tension;
- to change attitudes; and
- to instruct/teach.

You should always be prepared before chairing any meeting:

1 Know in advance what information, reports, agenda, layout, technical data or equipment is required.
2 Be clear about the purpose.
3 Inform other participants of the purpose and share, in advance, relevant information/documents.
4 Have a timetable and agenda (and notify others in advance).
5 Identify main topics with each having an objective.
6 Make necessary housekeeping arrangements.

Chairing a meeting means that you should guide and control it having defined the purpose of it, gatekeeping the discussions as appropriate (opening it to some, closing it when necessary), summarising, interpreting and concluding it with agreed decisions, on time.

The chairman's role in leading/refereeing effective meetings is to ensure that the following elements are handled correctly:

1 Aim – after starting on time, to outline purpose clearly.
2 Plan – to prepare the agenda (and allocate time).
3 Guide – to ensure effective discussion.
4 Crystallise – to establish conclusions.
5 Act – to gain acceptance and commitment and then to end on time.

Ask yourself

In my meetings, do I know the purpose, have an agenda, canvas opinions, agree conclusions and win acceptance of action needed?

Remember that meetings are groupings of people and can develop their own *personality*. It can help to understand the personality of a particular grouping by reference to group:

- conformity;
- values;
- attitude to change;
- prejudice; and
- power.

It follows that the method of running the meeting and making it effective depends on understanding and overcoming problems posed by the group personality.

Idea 100 – Communication within your organisation

Management mantra

Information should be treated as 'shareware'.

Organisations have a degree of permanence, hierarchy and formal communication. Informal communication supplements the formal communication that is needed in organisations.

The content of communication in organisations should be (in relation to):

1 The task:
- the purpose, aims and objectives;
- plans; and
- progress and prospects.
2 The team:
- changes in structure and deployment;
- ways to improve team work; and
- ethos and values.
3 The individual:
- pay and conditions;
- safety, health and welfare; and
- education and training.

The direction of flows of communication within an organisation must be downward, upward and sideways.

When forming decisions on what to communicate, bear in mind the *must-know* priorities and distinguish them from the *should-know* or *could-know* lower priorities. The best method for must-know items is face-to-face backed by the written word.

Two-way communication should be used and encouraged to:

- communicate plans/changes/progress/prospects;
- give employees the opportunity to change/improve management decisions (before they are made);
- use the experience and ideas of employees to the full; and
- understand the other side's point of view.

Ask yourself

Am I a good enough communicator? What do others think? Do I bother to find out, by communicating with them?

Summary and follow-up test

Summary

Personal reminders

Effective speaking – six key principles:

1 be clear;
2 be prepared;

3   be simple;
4   be vivid;
5   be natural; and
6   be concise.

Practical presentation skills require you to:

- profile the occasion, audience and location;
- plan and write the presentation;
- use visual aids (if appropriate);
- prepare your talk;
- rehearse (with others if necessary); and
- deliver on the day.

Good communicators are skilled at listening by:

- being willing to listen;
- hearing the message;
- interpreting the meaning;
- evaluating carefully; and
- responding appropriately.

Effective writing has three elements:

1   structure;
2   layout; and
3   style.

It also needs the six key principles of:

1 clarity;
2 planning;
3 preparation;
4 simplicity;
5 vividness;
6 naturalness; and
7 conciseness.

Follow-up test

- Have you identified and addressed communication/presentation strengths/ weaknesses of yourself and key members of your team?
- Can you calmly plan for meetings?
- Have meetings (one-to-one and others) improved?
- Has written communication improved your organisation?
- Has your performance as a communicator improved and do you listen more?

Index

appraisals 72–3

Belbin 101–2
brainstorming 114
  checklist 113
  follow-ups 112
  main steps 111
  rules 111
  successful 112
Buchan, John 75

Churchill, Sir Winston 155
communication 69, 78, 146
  creativity/innovation 102
  criticism
    giving 164
    receiving 164–5
  issues 147–8
  listening 149
    developing 151
    good 150
    poor 149–50
  meetings
    chairing 166–7
    needs 165
    preparation 166
    purpose 165–6
  one-to-one interviews 163–4
  open/constructive 107

organisational 168
  content 168
  direction 168
  must-know, should-know, could-know 169
personal skills checklist 148–9
presentations 157
  audience 158
  delivery 162
  location 158
  occasion 157
  planning/writing 159
  preparation 161
  rehearsal 161
  visual aids 160
reading
  good 151–2
  selective 152
  speed 152
speaking, principles 156–7
summary/follow-up test 169–71
writing
  business letters 154
  Churchill's guidelines 155
  effective 155–6
  elements 153
  principles 153
  reports 154–6
  rules 156
  style/tone 156

creativity
  encouraging   101–2
  obstacles   95–6
  overcoming obstacles   103
  recruiting/retaining   100–1
  stages   98
  stimulating   97–8
  suggestions   96–7
  summary/follow-up test
        118–19
  see also innovation

decision-making
  analytical ability   55–6
  compromise trap   55
  concept value   60–1
  conceptual thinking   58
  effective   50–1
    managers   53–4
    thinkers   51–3
  imagination   57–8
  intuition   59
  originality/innovation   59
  selecting/weighing-up options
        61–3
  summary/follow-up test
        89–90
  synthesis/holism   56–7
delegation   5, 17, 20
  checklist   19
  main reasons for not   18–19
  types of work   18
Drucker, Peter   7, 104

expectancy theory   124

feedback   102
  affirmative   136–7
  negative   137
  unnecessary   136
Ford, Henry   110
Four-D system (drop, delay, delegate, do)
        15–17

goals   6
  attaining   48–9
  integration of individual/organisational
        127
  long-term   10, 12
    personal life   11
    purpose of organisation   10
    purpose of own job   10
    where, what, how questions   11
  personal profile   45
  setting   12
    personal   46–7
    professional business   47–9
  setting realistic/challenging targets
        135–6
  short-term/medium-term   11
  smart   12–15
  summary/follow-up test   89

health management   21
  five-point test   21
  stress
    common roots   22–3
    indicators   21–2
    overcoming   23–4
Herzberg   127–30
hierarchy of needs   74–5, 125–6

ideas
  brainstorming 111–12
  choosing/refining 110
  recognising/selecting 110
  sieving 110
  sources 109–10
innovation
  business environment 104
    encouragement of teamwork 106
    flexible structure 105
    open/constructive communication
      107
    tolerant of failure 106
    top level commitment 104
  checklist 107–8
  communication as reinforcement 102
  key players 98
  management process 99
  overcoming obstacles 103
  requirements 99
  summary/follow-up test 118–19
  see also creativity
interviews 163–4

Jacob's ladder 135–6

Kouzes, James 75

leadership
  action-centred/functional approach
    36–7
  characteristics
    individual element 40
    tasks/qualities 38
    team element 39

defined 33
  qualities
    list 116–17
    rating 115–16
    summary/follow-up test 119–20
    testing 117–18
  short course on 79–80
  skills
    briefing 68–9
    controlling 70–1
    defining the task 64–6
    evaluating 71–4
    motivating 74–5
    organising 75–8
    planning 66–8
    setting an example 78–9
    summary/follow-up test 90–1
  summary/follow-up test 40–1
  teambuilding 81–3
  see also task, team, individual
    (circle model)

McGregor 126–7
management, defined 33
Maslow, A.H. 74, 125–6
meetings 165–7
  managing 26–7
  poor performance 6
  types 27–8
    advisory 28
    briefing 28
    committee 28
    council 28
    negotiating 28
    questions 27

motivation 78
  behavioural assumptions 126–7
  environment 139
  fair rewards 139–40
  feedback 136–7
  high 132
  inspirational leadership 75
  job satisfaction/dissatisfaction
       127–30
  maintain morale 137–8
  manager's checklist 130–1
  'Michelangelo motive'
       132–3
  personal 131–2
  principles 74
  recognition 141–2
  rules 123
       50:50 124
  satisfaction of needs 74–5, 125–6
  setting realistic/challenging targets
       135–6
  summary/follow-up test 142–3
  treat each person as individual
       133–4
motivation-hygiene theory
  good/bad feelings 127–8
  job dissatisfaction 128–9
  job satisfaction 129–30

objectives *see* goals
organisation 5
  interruptions 25
  meetings 26–8
  paperwork 25
  time management 26

Pareto principle 124
planning 48–9, 66–7
  checklist 67
  continuum 68
  medium-term 11
       smarter objectives 12–15
       successful 14–15
  short-term 11
  what, why, when, how, where
       questions 67
Posner, James 75
presentations 157–62

reward schemes 139–40

strategy 48–9

task, team, individual (circle model) 32
  achieving 32
  elements/variables 34
  expectations 34
  leadership/management integration 33
  needs 34, 35–6
  organising
       function 77
       skill/ability 76
teams
  appraising/training 72–3
  assessing consequences 71
  briefing 68–9
  encouraging innovation 106
  evaluating performance 71–2, 73
  judging 73
  maintain morale to maintain motivation
       137–8

size 78
teambuilding 91
  achieving the task 84
  decision-making skills 89–90
  developing the individual
    85–6
  individuals 88
  leadership 81–3, 90–1
  member functions 87
  processes 88
  questions concerning 85
  setting/achieving objectives 89
  summary/follow-up test 91
  team properties 87
  team roles 87
  teams within teams 88
Theory X and Y
  direction/control 126
  integration of individual/organisational
    goals 127
time management
  audit
    analyse/improve use of time 8
    identify activities 7–8
    keep daily record 7
    value other people's time 10
  basic approach 4
  committed 20
  delegate efficiently 17–20
  described 3
  failure to plan 3
  follow-up test 29–30
  health/stress 21–4
  identify long-term goals 10–12
  make medium-term plans 12–15
  organising 26
  principles 4, 29
  summary/follow-up test 29–30
  traps
    bad organisers 5
    delegation 5
    performance at meetings 6
    procrastination 5–6
    purposeless executive 6
  urgency/importance matrix 15–17
Tolman, Edward C. 124

Vroom, Victor H. 124

 **John Adair** is internationally recognized as a leadership and management guru and has twice been named as one of 40 people worldwide who have contributed most to the development of management thought and practice. He is the author of more than 30 books and numerous articles on history, leadership and management development and over two million people world-wide have participated in the Action-Centred Leadership training approach he pioneered. He became the world's first Professor of Leadership Studies, at the University of Surrey, and is currently Visiting Professor at the University of Exeter.

John Adair has worked with directors and senior managers as a consultant to a wide range of international organizations, including Shell, Exxon Chemicals, Mercedes-Benz and Unilever. He is currently an international management consultant advising a range of organizations spanning business, government, and the voluntary, education and health sectors.

Capstone Publishing (A Wiley company)
Tel: +44 (0) 1243 779777
Fax: +44 (0) 1243 770638
e-mail: info@wiley-capstone.co.uk
www.wileyeurope.com

Cover designed by Cylinder
Cover image © DigitalVision 2002

Printed in Great Britain